Psychotherapy
and the
Religiously Committed
Patient

Psychotherapy and the Religiously Committed Patient

E. Mark Stern, Editor

Iona College, New Rochelle, New York

C. 1985

The Haworth Press
New York

Psychotherapy and the Religiously Committed Patient has also been published as *The Psychotherapy Patient,* Volume 1, Number 3, Spring 1985.

The Haworth Press, Inc., 28 East 22 Street, New York, NY 10010

Library of Congress Cataloging in Publication Data
Main entry under title:

Psychotherapy and the religiously committed patient.

"Has also been published as the Psychotherapy patient, volume 1, no. 3, spring 1985"—T.p. verso.
    Includes bibliographies.
    1. Psychotherapy patients—Religious life—Addresses, essays, lectures.
2. Psychotherapy—Religious aspects—Addresses, essays, lectures.   3. Pastoral psychology—Addresses, essays, lectures. I. Stern, E. Mark, 1929- .
RC455.4.R4P792 1985   616.89'14   84-25276
ISBN 0-86656-394-6
ISBN 0-86656-396-2 (pbk.)

Psychotherapy and the Religiously Committed Patient

The Psychotherapy Patient
Volume 1, Number 3

CONTENTS

Introduction   xi

Psychotheology of Religious Commitment   1
    E. Mark Stern

    Psychotheological Foundations   1
    Commitment   1
    Patienthood   1
    The Role of the Psychotherapist   4
    Beyond Sanity   5
    Transformation of the Neurotic   10
    Psychotheological Conclusions   10

Lost in the No-Man's-Land Between Psyche and Soul   13
    Erika Wick

    The Case   14
    Key Issues   17
    Recommendations   22

Assessing Religious Maturity   25
    H. Newton Malony

    Underlying Assumptions   26
    Maturity Defined   28
    Religious Maturity and Treatment   30
    Dimensions Assessed   30
    Conclusion   32

The Religious Patient's Initial Encounter with Psychotherapy   35
   Carole A. Rayburn

  Introduction   35
  The Religiously Committed Patient   36

Forgiveness: A Spiritual Psychotherapy   47
   Kenneth Wapnick

Change in the Client and in the Client's God   55
   Albert S. Rossi

  The Case of Lisa   56
  Conclusion   61

**Latent Theology: A Clinical Perspective on *The Future
of an Illusion***   63
   Gary Ahlskog

**The Play of Illusion as an Opening to the Future of the Self:
Reflections of a Religious Clinician Occasioned by Rereading
*The Future of an Illusion***   71
   Vivienne Joyce

The Spiritual Emergency Patient: Concept and Example   79
   Steven J. Hendlin

  Research Supporting the Concept   80
  Toward a Definition   81
  Clinical Example of Spiritual Emergency   82
  Discussion and Final Comments   86

Formation Counseling   89
   Adrian van Kaam

  Formative Apprehension and Appraisal   89
  Emergence of the Need for Formation Counseling   90
  Formation Field   91
  Form Potencies   92
  Power of Emergent Formation Potencies   92
  Formation Counseling as Such   93
  Formative Dispositions and Expressions   94
  Formation Project   95
  Interformative Relationship   95
  Imposition of One's Own Form of Life   96
  Formation Counselor and Formation Traditions   97

Form Traditions of the Formation Counselor   99
Structure of the Interformative Relationship   100
Formative Disposition   101
Interformative Disposition   102
Principle of Interformation Applied to Counseling   103
Interformation as Participation in the Core Form   104
Free Participation of the Counselee in Interformation   105

Confrontation and the Religious Beliefs of a Client   **107**
    Samuel M. Natale

Confrontation   110

Metaphor and Therapy: Theory, Technique, and Practice
    of the Use of Religious Imagery in Therapy **117**
    Raymond J. Stovich

Theory: The Nature of Religious Language   117
Techniques: Working with Images   120

The Psychotherapist and Religious Commitment   **123**
    William N. Grosch

Dealing with Proceptive Countertransference-like Issues:
    The Factor of Psychotherapeutic Ideology   **129**
    Orlo Strunk, Jr.

The Nature of Ideology   129
Defenses Against Ideological Uncovering   130
Informing the Client of Psychotherapy as Ideology   131

Psychotherapy as a Religious Process: A Historical Heritage   **135**
    Hendrika Vande Kemp

Definitions   138
Psychotherapy as Sound Psychology, Sound Medicine, and
    Sound Religion   139
A Contested Divorce   140
Psychotherapy as a Religious Process   142
Conclusions   144

Initial Encounters of Religious and Priests with Psychotherapy   **147**
    Ann Marie Wallace

Background   147
Interviews   149
Conclusions   157

Introduction

The attainment of existential meaning foreshadows any commitment. Religious commitment is that coverall term dealing with the pursuance of a belief in the Thouness of the superindividual as well as with the sustaining motivation to follow through on the ethical and relational demands inherent in such a belief. As such, it emerges out of an intersubjective nexus—a term frequently used by Gabriel Marcel for the mysterious coupling which unites humanity and divinity. Since such linkages are fraught with fear and discontent, it is appropriate that religious commitment be seen as a patient attribute.

Religiously committed patients are often hooked into apprehensions of not being able to fulfill the external obligations and duties of a particular sectarian system. Yet they remain devoted to the experience of surrender and dedication to a divine will. It is within this surrender and dedication that the religiously committed patient needs to be addressed.

By and large, this collection of articles views the psychotherapeutic process as a means of enhancing commitment rather than merely as a way of abrogating pain and emotional discomfort. And since the religiously committed individual tends to regard experience as an approach to an essentially knowable Thou, therapeutic intervention tends to focus on the functions of faith and hope in the furtherance of existence.

As you read on, note the importance that many of the writers place on having psychotherapists who themselves have demonstrated religious commitment treat those with spiritual concerns. It may well be that such therapists are more inclined to regard a devout pathway as ontic reality rather than as the outline of a dysfunctional system. Regardless of who facilitates the therapeutic process, this issue of *The Psychotherapy Patient* strives to make clear that religious commitment, as an attribute of many who seek psychiatric or psychological help, involves a special sort of urgency that prompts a willingness to invoke faith as a central healing modality.

E. Mark Stern
Editor

Psychotherapy
and the
Religiously Committed
Patient

Psychotheology of Religious Commitment

E. Mark Stern

PSYCHOTHEOLOGICAL FOUNDATIONS

"To have a vocation or a religious stance" announced Jung (1954), is "to be addressed by a voice . . . whispering . . . new and wonderful paths" (p. 183). Emotional stability notwithstanding, experiencing this voice is learning to be responsively committed to what is most superindividual. For most religiously committed individuals, God is that given superindividuality. However, the prompting and subsequent responses to any committed search for inner meaning become the psychotheologic common ground of religion and psychotherapy. In this sense traditional religion speaks of the urgencies of the Creator while psychology confronts the experience of the inner voice and its attendant motivations. Within this resulting psychotheological sphere, these urgencies and aspirations provide the mainstream of inspiration.

COMMITMENT

Commitment in a psychotheological sense is the essence of one's life mission grounded in an I-Thou relationship. This dialogue between one's personal concerns and those of the other involves an intersubjective field of operation. It is this field or synthesis which forms the basis for the experience of the superindividual. Only as the other becomes Thou can there be any commitment. Thus committed experience is grounded within an interpersonal framework.

In this sense authentic religious commitment must transcend immediate or willful gratification because it is experienced beyond a narrow notion of self. As experience, religious commitment matures into existential courage—the willingness to be a whole self engaged within an interpersonal intersubjective mission (Tillich, 1952).

PATIENTHOOD

The religiously committed individual who seeks professional psychotherapeutic help is usually in the throes of a constant struggle to achieve the courage *to be* in the service of donating this being to a superindividual mission. Allowing the self to be and to become a part means the maintenance of a balance between finitude and one's place within the whole of creation. According to Andras Angyal (1965), "the self is a finite distance on an infinite line (since) . . . within the person each process or structure is part of a larger one" (pp. 298-299). Good psychotherapy enhances the patient's freedom to assert self while maintaining a sense of committed participation.

* * *

A medical student who had been raised in China by missionary parents reached an emotional impasse when she decided to challenge her mother's insistence that she too enter the foreign missions. For this woman it was less that she chose a secular avenue than that she learned to trust the promptings of her courage to go her own way.

* * *

A minister who had recently lost his wife and two children in a car crash began to appreciate the significance he had for several people who had been coming to him for spiritual guidance and counseling. This fact alone allowed him to come to terms with his chronic grief.

* * *

A religious woman ravaged with a progressive degenerative disease saw each outbreak of pain as an intensification of life. To her, pain became the essence of her participation in life.

* * *

Sandra had been married for a trifle over a year when Todd announced that he would not be accompanying her on an overseas business trip. Sandra flew to Paris alone but found the pain of estrangement too much to bear. She phoned me from Europe to tell me that not only was she losing Todd, but that her will to live was rapidly vanishing.

Sandra, who had recently become a Catholic, was not at all clear whether she had converted in order to please Todd's family. I suggested that, if she felt so inclined, she make use of her new religious potential. After all, regardless of what had prompted her move, the tenets of her belief were now her own. Sandra called me on Ascension Thursday, a day that has special significance for the Catholic Christian. On that day, the Paschal candle that has been present on the altar since Easter as the symbol of the risen Christ is removed, symbolizing the end of his earthly sojourn. According to the scripture reading of the day, "It is to your advantage that I go away, for if I do not go away, the Counselor will not come to you; but if I go, I will send him to you" (John 16:7). I enjoined the meaning of the day to help her see spiritual opportunity within abandonment. Together we spoke of the experience of abandonment in her life in the light of the missing Paschal presence.

By the time Sandra reached her next destination she had become aware that though Todd's loss was painfully consuming, she'd nevertheless come in contact with a level of solace she had obviously been seeking for many years. Her newfound religion had now become a mainstay of her emotional restoration.

* * *

Early in his ministry, a respected priest had spent the better part of a year on his back as part of the then accepted treatment regime for tuberculosis. Some 10 years later he became severely depressed. Despite intense psychotherapeutic intervention, accompanied by the judicious use of psychotropic drugs, Father Jones' depression became overwhelming.

In desperation, he asked to be reassigned to a distant city in hopes that his proximity to his parents' home would help reduce his inner ravages. Unexpectedly, both parents died within a year of his move. Father Jones chose to remain in his new parish but he remained clouded with avalanching depression. Yet, beyond his depression, he felt an unexplained ease about his parents' deaths. Inasmuch as they were older than most of his contemporaries' parents, he had, from early childhood, been haunted by the thought of their eventual deaths. Now, even in the depths of his own wilderness, he was grateful to God that his own pain seemed to make their departures bearable. Not long after their deaths, Father Jones succumbed to a massive coronary occlusion. Whatever the inner dynamics that may have contributed to his own early death, it seemed clear that, despite the pain, he had learned to get in touch with a growing meaning in his own depression. It had indeed motivated a final reunion.

Given the weight of his personal trials, perhaps other "healthier" solutions might have seemed more desirable. But for the committed religious person, God's purpose reigns in both fortune and misfortune. Certainly the anesthetic split of Father Jones' depression was decisive in his being able to deal with his parents' deaths. And yet these unhappinesses beg the issue since they easily confuse religious faith with the attainment of "happiness."

Despite the absence of obvious gratification, the issue at hand for the committed religious patient is the expectation of consolation evident in the manifestation of an intuitive cognitive process which Saint Thomas Aquinas declared was not to be equated with pure reason (*per modum cognitionis*) but rather with an unexpected presence of the transcendent beyond the self (*ipsum esse subsistus*) (Moglia, 1982, pp. 7-10). Saint

Augustine of Hippo noted that the human is "unknown even to his own self (knowing neither) what he may bear of what he may not bear . . . hidden from himself, but not from his Maker" (Augustine, 1958, p. 429). What power is there is known only on the level of unexpected consolation which for the committed religious person is usually coupled with a willingness to be addressed by that hidden voice referred to in the earlier reference to Jung.

In each of the above vignettes, each individual ultimately needed to reckon with manifestations of unexpected consolation or grace. The medical student found that even though not becoming a foreign missionary meant disappointing her parents, her courage helped her find her self-appointed place in the helping professions. The bereaved minister discovered that he could be sustained by his counselees. The woman weighed down by severe physical pain was able to use this pain as her entry into an aware universe. Sandra reached a sense of the meaning her new faith could have for her. It certainly might have been less ravaging had Sandra been able to have been "powerful" enough to effectuate a happier resolution in her marriage. And finally, Father Jones succeeded in detecting a spiritual essence in deep depression. The psychospiritual quests each of the individuals embarked on, although not always recognized as such, became the foci of each person's interplay between a gradually disclosed spiritual cognition and personal destiny, known in their minds only to their Source. For the committed religious person, this intimacy between soul and destiny is a spiritual advent.

THE ROLE OF THE PSYCHOTHERAPIST

In working with the religiously committed psychotherapy patient, the therapist serves as the person facilitating the development of a correspondence between spiritual purpose and human acceptance. Acceptance, as both human endurance and personal fallibility, serves as the foundation of spiritual illumination. The facilitation extends to, but is not limited to, the quest for spiritual luminescence and sustenance.

"Signals of transcendence within the empirically given human situation" (Berger, 1969, p. 65) means looking beyond mundane bounties and boundaries. Because of this goal, the religiously committed person may appear like a stranger to the secular psychotherapist. The haphazard marriage between pastoral theology and many schools of psychotherapy has recently formed an as-yet uneasy truce between the two. But in their ideals, each is in a position to address the issue of a misused faith. Yet the fear of ceremonial violations and moral oversights are variously seen by the religious and nonreligious psychotherapist as developmental issues—needing to be seen within the light of emerging maturity. In this sense the struggle between sanctity and sanity is relative. The ongoing challenges for all psychotherapists working with religiously committed patients involve a great interpersonal and intersubjective sensitivity and a strong respect for the development of a meaningful purpose in life.

BEYOND SANITY

Sanctity for the Christian is not identical with sanity nor is moral perfection identical with a response to the Divine will. For the committed Christian patient, sanctification remains inscrutable. To be precise, it becomes a happening in God's order poised between holiness and sinfulness (Beirnaert, 1964). Within this balance choice may be possible, though pride and moralistic self-sufficiency hinder such choices. Even if the individual does yield to what he or she may consider a higher calling, feelings of abandonment and sin may still abound. Nor is the religious journey limited by such feelings. As stated by Van de Meersch (cited in Beirnaert), "In this outcast, in this adulterer, in this homosexual, yes, say it boldly, there is still enough to make for a saint, even if it is too late for him to be henceforth anything else but an outcast, an adulterer, a homosexual" (p. 147).

Reflecting this position, the religiously committed patient can reach some level of emancipation *in consequence of* the outcast state. Despite woe, misery, and anguish, illumination and unexpected consolation may be experienced within religious commitment. Such was Gloria's lot.

The Case of Gloria

Gloria was urged to consult me by an elderly nun who served as her spiritual director. The director was the prioress of a small contemplative monastery to which Gloria, because of her abundant personality problems, had been denied entry. I was initially impressed by Gloria's expressionless face. There had been little ease for this 28-year-old woman who probably hadn't smiled since childhood and who expressed disgust for her body. She was preoccupied with concealing her breasts under a heavy knitted woolen sweater which she wore throughout the entire winter and spring. Nor could she comfortably look at others—reflexively lowering her gaze in order to avoid eye/body contact. Her disappointment was exceptionally profound on learning that she would not be allowed to enter the contemplative order.

For months after our initial contact Gloria would not speak above a whisper. When asked how she felt about being rejected by the contemplative order, Gloria indicated that she had no legitimate right to be regretful, or angry. It was obvious that any constructive attempt to make sense out of her present existence would be long in coming.

Gloria had been raised in the lap of material luxury. Her father had been a prominent attorney, her mother a self-described "club woman." The two younger brothers had successfully followed their father's career while Jill, the youngest in the family, was married to a foreign-service officer and had long since lived abroad.

It was Gloria's eighth-grade parochial-school teacher who had initially encouraged her to enter the aspirants' program—a boarding school sponsored by the nuns whose religious order worked in her parish. Her parents strongly objected, and instead sent their daughter to an international school in Switzerland. Nominal Catholics themselves, they hoped to dissuade their daughter's growing religious preoccupations.

While in Switzerland, Gloria became friendly with the school's laundress, whose household she described as extremely poor—"sans un sou." Nevertheless, Gloria treasured the many hours spent with the laundress and her family. So close was this bond that the school gave her permission to spend occasional weekends with her "Swiss family." Gloria was impressed by the overall piety of this financially needy household. As a result, she became increasingly aware that despite the good fortunes of her own family, she herself was left with a sense of abject futility. It was obvious that Gloria's desire for a life of renunciation and poverty was further enhanced by the love and welcome offered her by the laundress's family. Yet this desire could not have been so crucial were it not for her romance with the idea of a consecrated religious life.

Back in the United States, Gloria attended a series of retreats sponsored by several contemplative religious orders. Her emotional instability must have been striking because each of the Sisters charged with screening new vocations wasted little time in suggesting that she seek psychological help.

Gloria, now resigned to not entering the convent, presented herself for psychotherapy. What, I asked, were her ideas about her having been spurned so often? Rejection had finally become the metaphor for her whole life. Even so, she willingly saw the hand of God at work—obvious even in the sadness dating back to early childhood.

Though resigned to not being a nun, Gloria remained cautious about miscasting those who had rejected her applications in an angry light. Nevertheless, she did feel misunderstood, if not completely cast aside. Inasmuch as she had trouble going beyond her hurt, I asked if being misunderstood was, for her, an inevitable Christian penance.

Gloria could not immediately respond, but sessions appeared to highlight her disquietude. Yet, for her, pain was the evidence of a worthy struggle. As bonding, the challenge of pain drew her close to a deeply felt religious commitment which for her entailed a significant degree of ac-

ceptance of what she considered to be God's will. Not unlike the sentiments so eloquently expressed by the poet-priest Gerard Manly Hopkins,

> What I know of thee I bless,
> As acknowledging thy stress
> On my being as seeing
> Something of thy holiness.

True to this sentiment, Gloria's feelings of loss and abandonment were,
for her, analogous to Christ's kinship with isolation and loneliness in
Gethsemane. Within this identification with her Lord's struggle, life for
Gloria became both mission and calling. It remained the therapeutic task
to help interlink this identification with her spiritual and emotional development.

Gloria's maturation was slow in coming. She feared both the dangers
and the delights of her impulses. She was justifiably concerned that, left
unguarded, her rage would be consciously aimed at those several nuns
and priests whose role was significant in her having been rejected from a
vowed contemplative life. This Gloria associated with the danger of losing her faith. Yet she was somewhat aware that the boundaries of this
faith needed to be redefined. On some levels this terror needed to be seen
as an authentic challenge, ultimately serving as a maturational pathway to
her learning to make decisions on her own. And while this could be
dangerous, it could serve as her rite of passage in learning to revere *her
own* inner authority. Ultimately, the attainment of this personal authority,
in concert with several other responsible developments, resulted in
Gloria's allowing herself the right to design her own religious vocation.
She eventually made private vows of dedication, which she saw as her
license to work with the poor and downtrodden.

In short order, Gloria found her way to a group of self-proclaimed
Catholic anarchists who had for several decades dedicated themselves to
housing, feeding, and clothing the needy. As anarchists, each person
exercised responsibility for his or her specialized mission. For Gloria,
this meant working with a soup kitchen on skid row. Given this new development in her life, the thrust of Gloria's psychotherapy focused on her
coming to terms with mistrust. As in the past, there were fears of her
parents whisking her away—fears presently inspired by a series of well-
publicized anti-cult kidnappings. When asked why they would act so pre-
cipitously, Gloria presumed it was because of their suspicions of her being a lesbian. I asked her if she considered herself a lesbian, but soon it
became clear that she didn't fully understand all the implications of the
term "lesbian." To her, lesbianism was somehow related to her continuing fears about exposing the shape of her breasts, resulting in defensive obsession with wearing bulky male pullovers. She dated this ob-

session to being frightened off at the onset of puberty when her father had made what seemed to her to have been a semi-suggestive sexual comment. In later years she became concerned that she would be in a state of mortal sin if she allowed priests or nuns to see the outline of her breasts.

For years there had been haunting nightmares portraying her being sexually abducted by a figure she saw as the devil. Feeling the victim of demonic possession, she sought out a charismatic healing team consisting of a priest and several lay members. It was her hope that they might help "deliver" her from evil thoughts. The priest, a trained pastoral counselor, urged her to follow up on the healing prayers by carefully attending to her psychotherapy. This voice of authority became a turning point in her therapy. A new level of hope was dawning, matched in force by direct transferential fears that I might be an unknowing instrument of the devil.

"And what would the devil want with you?" I asked. Gloria moved to cross her arms over her breasts. I continued, "I guess you feel that once we focus on sexuality the devil finds himself in these sessions."

Gloria acknowledged her fascination with this fright. "Not that you would make any abusive moves," she tried to reassure herself. Then followed, "I'm just never sure if I don't make people feel uncomfortable." Soon afterward Gloria acknowledged her dread of being abandoned by me because of her "impure" and "objectionable" thoughts. I asked her if it was her impure thoughts or the *objections* she felt that I, like her parents, might be having about her having to come to terms with being a woman.

It would take some time for Gloria to integrate my query. In the meantime, she felt that she may have outmaneuvered Christ with her persisting sexual thoughts. Could it be that her terror of her breasts was the source of a tormented Christ? But as she reached for some foothold on sanity, she reminded herself that Jesus was known to cavort with "fallen" women. Later she spoke of her mother's near-phobic cautiousness. She knew from her mother that she would remain "bad" if she failed to confess *all* of her "impure sexual thoughts" prior to her First Holy Communion at age seven. Her fear of sinning took the form of a compulsion urging her to hallucinate sexual organs on the statues depicting the Holy Family. Even after psychotherapy there would be fears that sexual obsessions could surface at any time.

Beyond such terrors Gloria needed a better understanding of "exposure." Shades of being "caught" in an incestuous pact with her father seemed disproportionately powerful measured against her quest for union with Christ. As she became more involved in therapy, shame showed itself as panic threatening to leave her powerless and impulse ridden. Yet it remained her obligation to herself to begin to reckon with all of her emerging fears even as they included the several "objectionable" parts of herself. As this reckoning proceeded, breasts and emotional exposure needed to be incorporated into a full picture of self. In the quest for some unification of who she was, Gloria needed to feel appropriate even through the darkest side of her fears. A developed self, I explained, was one way of dealing with her obsessional terror of sin. Our work had become a balancing act through which she could better distinguish between her need for a sense of self and the terror of falling apart.

Gloria's potential for making the best use of her emerging maturity was getting into focus. Up to now all power depended on her weakness, but weakness that turned into a special strength within the family. Recall that her insecure and jealous mother often accused the child Gloria of having the power to threaten her parents' marriage. Yet, in a comparable vein, Gloria probably kept the marriage intact by serving as the necessary wedge between them. In having become the easy scapegoat within her family, Gloria could only interpret each of her parent's approaches to her as frightening. Even Gloria's religiously linked obsessiveness provided a *noli tangere*—do not touch—motto. But beyond the linkage with the family system, Gloria's dedication to religion had finally become more than a way of distracting from the family's problems. Her mystical bent was also her personal pathway, thus charging her therapy with a task. Included in that task was the development of a commitment to be a self who could be increasingly responsive to the superindividual. Responsiveness to the superindividual developed into a further commitment to the spirit of the Christian anarchist community she had chosen.

Gloria's rejection from contemplative orders finally provided her with an opportunity and foundation for setting herself apart from the emotional ravages of her highly enmeshed family of origin. Her fears of being possessed—at first by father and later by devil—began to give way, thus forging a new link to a community of committed believers.

This new link demanded that Gloria relinquish the strangulating ties to her family so that she might achieve some measure of emotional freedom. For Gloria, this freedom meant allowing herself the right to an appropriate spiritual calling. In order for her to rally newer levels of intersubjectivity, Gloria needed to release herself from stereotypic role assignments. Such liberation, when truly achieved, becomes the cornerstone of grace.

For Gloria, the attainment of freedom helped her bear greater witness to the unexpected presence of the transcendent—or movement beyond self (*ispum esse subsistus*). Her destiny had finally become a spiritual advent. Her growing ability to outpace morbidity allowed her to recognize the good hidden within evil. Eventually her life became integrated.

As each element within this integration began to provide a frame of reference, Gloria was able to see her life as a vital contribution to the superindividual. As an expression of her deepest religious sensibilities, Gloria was able to experience this contribution as communion with the Thou. Cooperation/communion of self and other extended Gloria's creative potential. False self gave way to a truly participatory self. ''Two beings

remain two and yet are one by participation in each other'' (Rahner &
Vorgrimler, 1965, p. 337).

TRANSFORMATION OF THE NEUROTIC

For Gloria and other religiously committed patients, transformation of
neurotic destiny is more than psychological cure. It is a realized fellowship with the superindividual. In this sense, fellowship becomes the experience of belief, conferring a developing personal relationship with the
Creator. This relationship interfaces with new scopes of emotional organization. A new self comes into being granting all that is good for the person.

Even dysfunctional neurotic patterns serve the good as launching pads.
Through their offices, the believer begins to visualize what is possible,
even though it be "through a glass darkly." For Gloria, this process involved learning to regard all stages of her struggle as providing insight
and redemption. She needed to look back on each of these stages as
various means of amending her life while enduring its consequences. In
the same vein, recall the painful experience of the woman with the degenerative disease cited earlier in this article. Difficult as her discomforts
had been, they became the foundations for her growing pains in the developing life of the spirit. Similarly, the minister who suffered the loss of his
wife and two children was finally able to witness the transformation of his
grief into a longing to remain available to the service of others.

What was transformed in all three cases gave birth to new adaptations
and values—each bearing a special relationship to the superindividual.
And as creations of this superindividuality they fostered a growing intimacy between self and spiritual destiny. Recall that emotional dysfunction is the product of stereotyped narrow functioning meant to seal
fate, whereas spiritual awakening opens the self to productive levels of
participation. This awakening may take place as the psychotherapist bears
witness to that which is authentic within the dysfunctional stalemate.
Gloria's therapeutic development was both metaphor and fact of her
spiritual growth. As her therapist I was responsible for witnessing her
struggles as they interfaced with her leaps toward an intimacy with the
superindividual.

PSYCHOTHEOLOGICAL CONCLUSIONS

As self moves into soul, movement finally reaches the mystery of existential freedom. The attainment of such freedom can be realized within
the psychotherapeutic enterprise as both patient and therapist confirm the

expansive potential. Only then are psychological and theological insights melded into a unified approach to the emotionally entrapped patient.

Patients need to know that their respective quests are honored by the therapists they have chosen. As witnesses to psychological growth and expansiveness, psychotherapists take on the mantle of psychological as well as spiritual authority (Stern & Marino, 1970). Beholding their patients' lives as radically developmental leads to a better understanding of a covenant with God's evolutionary essence within personal experience. This process is sacred since any insights a patient receives are more than an elaboration of individual psychodynamics. These insights establish a basis for the appreciation of the whispering voice of revelation making each pilgrimage into patienthood a confirmation of the worthwhileness and sacredness of the community of all human life.

REFERENCES

Angyal, A. (1965). *Neurosis and treatment: A holistic theory* (E. Haufmann & R.M. Jones, Eds.). New York: John Wiley & Sons.

Augustine: An Augustine synthesis (E. Przywara, Arranger). (1958). New York: Harper Torchbook.

Beirnaert, L. (1964). Does sanctification depend on psychic structure? In W. Birmingham & J.E. Cunneen (Eds.), *Cross currents of psychiatry and Catholic morality*. New York: Pantheon.

Berger, P. (1969). *A rumor of angels*. New York: Doubleday.

Jung, C.G. (1954). The development of the personality. *Collected Works* (Vol. 17). New York: Pantheon, Bollingen Series.

Moglia, P. (1982). My experience of God or my experience of me. *Contemplative Review, 15*(1), 7-10.

Rahner, K. & Vorgrimler, (1965). *Theological dictionary* (R. Strachan, Trans.). New York: The Seabury Press.

Stern, E.M. & Marino, B. (1970). *Psychotheology: The discovery of sacredness in humanity*. Paramus, NJ: Paulist Press.

Tillich, P. (1952). *The courage to be*. New Haven, CT: Yale University Press.

Lost in the No-Man's-Land Between Psyche and Soul

Erika Wick

Although it appears that there is therapeutic territory that might rightfully be claimed by both professionals—the psychotherapist and the clergy—it may come somewhat as a surprise that some of that territory has turned into a no-man's-land rather than being a shared or competitively occupied zone. A major area in this zone of bilateral withdrawal is the area of clinical problems related to the value field. Since values are social-reference-system-interrelated (Wick, 1983), leaving a client troubled in this area without a support system can amount to endangering the individual and potentially others as well. Serious value problems readily turn into existential problems and, without help, present or ensuing experiences of despair tend to be followed by destructive actions. Considering the seriousness of the issue, how then is it possible that neither professional group is committed to this value no-man's-land?

Psychotherapists have for long been indoctrinated to believe that psychotherapy ought to be value free. Ideally this means that psychotherapy should be nonjudgmental, and responsive to the client's values and to the needs resulting from the person's value system, rather than a process of converting the client to the values held by the therapist. In order for the therapist to understand the client's value system and how it functions, the professional needs to be knowledgeable in the area of values. However, because of the myth of value-free psychotherapy, psychotherapists have not been trained in dealing with values. Therapists have been led to believe that conflicts over value issues should either be denied their legitimacy and relegated to the realm of the neurotic/histrionic, or that the client should be referred to the value expert, the clergy, or to a specifically trained pastoral counselor.

The clergy on the other hand, the experts on morality, may have plenty of information available on philosophical and theological relevance of values, but, having been trained in pastoral counseling by mental health

Erika Wick received her PhD in 1964 from the University of Basel, Switzerland. She has been professor of psychology at St. John's University, Jamaica, New York, since 1976 and has been affiliated with the Vietnam Veterans Outreach Center in Queens, New York, since 1982.

professionals who were fairly ignorant about the clinical significance of moral development, they tend to be equally lost when it comes to helping a client with serious psychological symptomatology related to values. A clergyperson's expertise tends to be most effective within the moral reference system that his or her religion provides. The moral-psychological understanding of the religious leader is normally related to issues of moral-code compliance and conflicts resulting from transgressions of stated values as well as the difficulties a believer may experience in accepting sometimes outdated and no longer viable values, which a religion has not yet discarded, such as the Catholic "moral" value of going along with nature's fertility selection as opposed to the "immoral" act of fertility selection by reason.

In view of this, the therapist's move to refer a client for pastoral help as soon as a value issue is raised seems to be overly simplistic. Will the member of the clergy be equipped to handle the problem in question? Or will the client get lost in the no-man's-land extending between the territory of the caretaker of the soul and the territory of the caretaker of the psyche?

The following case discussion illustrates the point made. It is the story of a veteran of the Vietnam war, who did get lost in the no-man's-land between psyche and soul. After his experience with the pastoral and the mental health professionals he vowed never to see a priest or a psychotherapist again.

THE CASE

When John came to the Vietnam Veterans Outreach Center it was not voluntary. He was under pressure. After John had been involved in some serious acting out his employer threatened to fire him if he kept refusing to seek help.

The presenting symptomatology revealed that this veteran suffered from a post-traumatic stress disorder aggravated by a value-related condition, not classified in the DSM III.

The following is a selective recount of John's personal history, focusing on issues and events relevant to the development of this condition. Some factual details have been changed to protect the client from being identified. The psychological facts have not been altered. John's story reflects experiences shared by many veterans.

John, the son of a World War II veteran, had grown up in a traditional Catholic environment. When John joined the Marines his family was supportive. The parish priest blessed him; and the United States government left no doubt that the war he was going to fight was for a just and noble cause: namely, to fight communism, to preserve freedom and democracy, and to assist an oppressed people. The Marine Corps echoed the government's proclamation in its own amplified version. Despite the war protests John never doubted the rightfulness of the government's action. He was going to serve in Vietnam "for God and country." John's peers organized a good-bye party for him and sent him off with pride. The young marine perceived himself as an ambassador of freedom sent by the American people. He sensed their appreciation of his willingness to put his life on the line.

In Vietnam John quickly became involved in heavy combat, and the alternative, "kill or be killed," took precedence over any speculations about the moral justification of killing. Soon, though, a few issues became puzzling: The war effort did not seem to be one of clear goal direction. The effort did not seem to aim at winning, restoring democracy, and getting the killing over with. Too many times after a hill had been taken, the troops were pulled back only to return a few days later. More comrades would lose their lives trying to regain control over the same territory. Then there were the exclusionary zones which were not temples, churches, or hospitals. Rumor had it that these areas were excluded from destruction because they were of economic interest to an engineering company in which influential Americans were stockholders. The company flourished while it supported the war effort. The end of the war was not in the company's interest. There were more rumors. All seemed to promote the theory of an economic reason for the war. In the meantime John lost a few close friends and finally he had to stand by helplessly as his closest buddy died. John began to hear the news about war protests in the United States with a different ear. Maybe not all of the protesters were sissies and traitors. As John lost faith in the cause of the war, doing his job became increasingly harder. He finally went to see the chaplain. The man of God dismissed his concerns and admonished him to fight more fiercely. "Kill as many as you can," he said.

Finally John came home. Nobody gave him a hero's welcome. Nobody said: "Let's celebrate the good job you have done over there." Instead, after he returned to American soil, he was immediately insulted by some peace activists. He had barely stepped off the plane when he was attacked verbally, spit at, and even slapped with a newspaper by a young woman. He was called a baby-killer and a murderer. Some activists ridiculed him. Some cited slogans like "fighting for peace is like fucking for virginity." His parents and the whole family were happy to see John back alive. However, they had, just as John himself, increasingly grown disillusioned with the war and were not so sure anymore that John had gone through the hardships he had endured to create a better world for mankind. His old peers seemed to avoid John. Although nobody spelled it out for John, he got the message that he was no longer one of them. He started to feel like a leper. John tried to get a job. Many prospective employers seemed to become fearful when they found out John had been involved in heavy combat. To them he was a trained killer. Finally, with the help of a concerned veteran, the ex-marine found work. There have never been any complaints about the quality of his performance.

In the meantime the U.S. government pulled out of Vietnam. John certainly was for ending the war, any war. But he could not follow the government's logic. "Peace with honor" was the issue at hand. But peace with honor could have been had a few years and almost 60,000 American soldiers' lives ago. Was fighting communism, establishing democracy and freedom, and helping an oppressed people no longer worth killing or dying for? And if it was not now, had it ever been? Was killing for freedom good and right only while it was supported by public opinion? Did morality hinge on a popular vote? Next, the draft evaders were pardoned. Had they been right in the first place? Then the Vietnam veterans' memorial was built. President Reagan, referring to the names of the fallen soldiers said: "I *think* the names that are being read are of men who died for freedom . . ." Wouldn't a president know for sure? And Caspar Weinberger, the Secretary of Defense, by saying "that we should never again ask our men and women to serve in a war which we do not intend to win," confirmed on national television what had been one of John's worst fears, namely, that the war had been a game.

John was glad to find that his father understood him. But in his struggle to restore the war to a moral enterprise, the father's comment was no help: "We may just as well face it," the elder said, "it looks like you've been had."

John tried to keep to himself that he was a haunted man. The memories and nightmares, the flashbacks on rainy and foggy nights, depression, fits of anger often directed at innocent bystanders, suicidal impulses, the desire to blow up the whole world got John to see a psychotherapist. The therapist was willing to help him with his depression, his rages, and his fear of getting involved in some violent acting out. But when John brought up his moral conflicts over the war and over having killed in Vietnam, although never outside of necessity or frivolously, the psychiatrist referred him to his pastor. The priest, in turn, referred him back to his therapist. He explained that he had previously dealt with felons and murderers, but never with anybody who had killed more than two people. "You are a mass murderer. I cannot help you. You have to get professional help."

John became agitated. He went for a long walk. As he walked he heard the chaplain say, "Kill as many as you can"; then the pastor, "You are a mass murderer"; then the chaplain again, "kill"; the pastor, "mass murderer." And on it went: "Kill, mass murderer, kill, kill as many as you can. . ." Right then John felt, he could do it. He could kill them all . . . all, all, all, including himself.

John did not go back to his therapist. Instead he vowed never to see a priest or a psychiatrist again.

KEY ISSUES

The case of the veteran reported here clearly involves value issues, in fact, complex value issues, but by no means issues that should be beyond the competence of a trained mental health professional. This does not mean that the assistance of the clergy might not be desirable at some point in the therapeutic process. On the other hand, we may ask, should a member of the clergy be able to assist a parishioner with the problems delineated here? Reasonably, it cannot be expected that a priest would be able to deal with all the issues involved, but he should be able to zoom in on the—albeit few—religiously bound moral-authority-related issues and offer the means religion affords to bring about healing, rather than rejecting and judging the person seeking help. Yet, in the actual case, both professionals were reluctant to work with the client who had a value problem. Could it be that they did not reject a client, but that they both rejected a problem they did not know how to deal with? While psycholinguistics creates the impression that the value field is "occupied" by religion (compare, e.g., sin, repentance, confession), closer scrutiny reveals that only a small fraction of the area is mapped out by the alleged value experts. Most of the value field is a no-man's-land, open for exploration.

One of the difficulties the clergy as well as the psychotherapists seem to experience, when confronted with clients who have value problems, is the fact that value-related problems have generally not been well defined. Some value issues have been addressed within the framework of certain concepts of a given religion, but were never generalized to the format of psychological conceptualizations. In order to bring some clarification to the value field, a few symptomatic pictures shall be identified so that the professional may be able to sort out and label a problem, rather than feel puzzled when clients present themselves overwhelmed with clashing values, value conflicts, value confusion, and ready to reject all values, while totally distrusting all value authorities.

There is not enough space here to analyze the veteran's case in depth, identifying all of the value issues involved. And a cursory review of the case would not shed any light on the value field. Compromising between both approaches, a few key issues will be listed and one of them will be dealt with in greater detail. Hopefully this initial presentation will serve as a basis for further exploration of the value field.

Among the key issues that need to be explored in the case of this veteran are the following: (1) significant value reference systems (the relevant moral authorities and the stage of moral development); (2)

diagnosing conditions related to value conflict; (3) guilt issues: guilt and responsibility (accepted values), guilt and causality, guilt by accusation (a) external (the others) (b) internal (guilt feelings, emotions, nightmares, flashbacks, etc.), collective guilt; (4) forgiving and forgiveness (e.g., forgiving oneself for letting oneself be used, forgiving those who did not ask for it, the economy of forgiveness); (5) integrity and self-esteem (being the blamed victim: "murderer" (Ryan 1971), and so forth.

This is an incomplete list. Nevertheless, it reflects to some degree the density of the psychological presence in the value field. Actually, no matter who identifies, promotes, and reinforces values, be it a political, cultural, or religious group, the underlying individual functioning patterns of value-acquisition, -retention, -change, -transgression, -readjustment, and so forth, always follow psychological laws.

The one key issue that will be discussed in greater depth is diagnosing conditions related to value conflicts and value discrepancies. Labeling these conditions is possible, because these conditions follow predictable psychological patterns. Once a therapist has established the parameters of a client's value conflicts and/or value confusion, then it becomes much easier to develop realistic therapeutic strategies. Four diagnostic categories are proposed in the hope that they will be useful to therapists and clergy.

First the necessary terms will be clarified and then the veteran's case will be reviewed from a value-related diagnostic viewpoint.

The following theoretical considerations will focus on a limited number of syndromes which either apply in this case or are useful in delineating related syndromes with similar symptomatology. The following will be identified: anomia, antinomia, polynomia, and transnomia.

An *antinomia* is the psychological condition which may ensue when a person is confronted with an antinomy. In law an antinomy (nomos = law in Greek) is the paradox which is created either by "a contradiction in the law, or between two equally binding laws" or principles or by "an authoritative contradiction" (Oxford Universal Dictionary, 1964, p. 76). Corresponding contradictions do occur in the realm of moral laws and ethics and can have a considerable effect on a person's value system. The impact of a moral antinomy can cause any shade of consequence from having no effect on a person's value system—if the value discrepancy is judged to be trivial and of no existential relevance—all the way to a total value-system collapse, completely destabilizing an individual—if the value clashes are perceived as major and if the person has a major existential investment in the value(s) involved. The value crisis focuses on a conflict of values which had been understood to be stable and noncontradictory. However, through value-authority action, the values have been changed suddenly or over time (abortion is murder, then is legal; killing in war is moral, then is immoral), or because the authority concurrently supports contradictory values (use of coercion to enforce democracy) or because value-authority representatives within the same value system contradict each other (two priests of the same church). In summary: An antinomia is a disturbing psychological condition that develops in response to a value contradiction that occurs through a value shift or is proclaimed from within an intact value reference system creating value clashes and value confusion.

An *anomia* comes about when one sets oneself up as the sole value authority in defiance of socially accepted norms and values, be it because such values were never acquired or because previously accepted values were subsequently discarded. The anomic condition in itself is stable. The conflict between individual and societal values is perceived as a problem from a societal viewpoint (danger of criminal acting out), while the discrepancy between individual and societal values are not disturbing to the anomic. Examples of anomic individuals are the psychopath who never acquired a set of socially accepted values and the disillusioned person who, after a precipitating event, discarded previously held social values.

Polynomia is the condition marked by considerable upset and destabilization which may follow a person's exposure to, or more likely serious involvement with, social reference systems which promote values different from or outright contradictory to his or her own. The value systems and reference systems involved appear to be stable within themselves. The value discrepancies are discovered through the individual's move(s) between reference systems. Examples: Value discrepancies are encountered between value systems held by different cultures, social classes, religions, and so forth. In culture shock there may be a value involvement on a polynomic level; or a marriage to a husband of a different religion who expects compliance with his value system, which contradicts the wife's own value set, can push the wife into a state of polynomia.

Transnomia is the condition that may arise in conjunction with a value crisis which is due to a normal developmental transition between stages of moral development. In-between-stage phases result from the shifts in psychosocial reference systems, which also function as value reference systems (Wick, 1983). These transitional phases are marked by value instability. Old values are destabilized, questioned, and possibly discarded. New values are not yet firmly rooted and have not yet been sufficiently tested to build a firm value basis. The transnomic person is rattled by value insecurity and value confusion, as previously stable values emerge as unstable, unsettled by discrepancies and contradictions, stemming from two competing value systems which partially overlap and partially leave gaps in between them. Example: Adolescents involved in the process of shifting from a traditional value-reference system to a peer value-reference system, trying to shed parental values while acquiring peer values, may become sufficiently upset over value conflicts to qualify as transnomics.

Table 1 summarizes the differences between the value related conditions.

The veteran's case will now be reviewed in terms of the conditions identified.

John's experiences with his moral reference groups were puzzling and destabilizing. Initially the focus was on killing as a moral issue; later the morality of the moral authorities became an equally burning issue.

Originally John had been brought up to believe that killing was bad. Then his mind was reconditioned to accept that killing in a war could be well justified. He fought in a war that was portrayed as noble and "good." He killed. And after the dirty job was done he was faced with changed values. The killing, after the fact, was labeled "bad" and John was rejected as a "murderer."

Table 2 lists John's experiences of the value switching as it was projected by the different moral reference authorities.

John, the "innocent warrior" made into a "murderer," was faced with a moral antinomy. Yet his antinomia developed slowly over time. Much of his learning about the value switching was gradual. At the beginning John even discounted negative value messages reaching him directly, such as the insults by the peace activists at the airport. He excused them as single individuals' aberrations. Only slowly did he begin to understand that the values had changed. At that time, when John still had hope that his moral value confusion could be resolved and the stress-disorder symptoms ameliorated, he sought professional help. Society's sanctioned healer refused to touch the value issue. And the priest, calling him

TABLE 1

A table summarizes the differences between the value related conditions.

condition	value systems	value stability	value discrepancy
transnomia	two competing systems	values stable within system	values clashing during transition from old to new value system
antinomia	one value system	value clashing within system	value contradiction within same system
anomia	one value system	stable value system	stable a- or anti-social system – conflicts when clashing with social systems
polynomia	two or more coexisting systems	values stable within system	exposure to different value system(s) creates value contradiction

TABLE 2

MORAL STATUS	
before and/or during tour of duty	**after** the war
1. **traditional reference system** A. nuclear reference system *a. parents, family* "for God and country" **+**	**—** "it looks like you've been had"
B. extended reference system *b. God, church* parish priest: "God bless our warrior" **+** chaplain: "kill as many as you can"	**—** pastor: "you are a mass murderer"

c. US government, US Marine Corps
"moral war"   **+**
  fight communism and oppression
  preserve freedom and democracy
	— "police action", no declared war
	pull out of Vietnam (freedom and democracy
	    no longer worth dying or killing for?)
	pardon draft evaders (had they been right
	    in the first place?)
	"war, we never intended to win" Casper
	    Weinberger (a killing game?)
	"I think . . . were fighting for freedom"
	    Ronald Reagan (wouldn't he know
	    for sure?)

2. **contemporary reference system** A. nuclear reference system *a. peers* "we're rooting for you, we're proud of you" **+**	**—** "you are no longer one of us"

B. extended reference system
b. the others (general public, vox populi)
"we stand behind our soldiers,   **+**
  you are going on our behalf,
  thanks for putting your life on the line"
	— spit at, insulted, humiliated
	  "babykiller, murderer"
	  "no jobs for you, we are afraid of you"

3. **self-reference system**
"for God and country"   **+**
  for freedom and democracy
  against communism and oppression
	? was it a bad war?
	  was killing murder?

a mass murderer, irrevocably confronted him with the reality of the antinomy, which so far he had tried to ignore or negate. When the representative of church and God proclaimed war killing murder, the authorities' switching of values, the blatant value contradiction could no longer be denied. This triggered a serious state of antinomia. John faced total value confusion, as good and bad turned into changeable commodities depending on their usefulness to untrustworthy authorities. His insight was gained at the price of total disillusionment and was followed by a full collapse of his value system. John's value-related sense of direction in life was thwarted and his sense of hopelessness led to utmost existential despair. After war injuries had left John's body partially disabled, society now even stripped him of his integrity and labeled him a criminal. John was not sure anymore whether it was desirable to be a moral man in this "moral" society. Instead, he angrily embraced his status of society reject and, retrogressively discarding values and value reference authorities, reached a state of anomia. Once there, he reestablished values in accordance with his own selfish interests and convenience and without concern for social norms. He was now the only acceptable moral authority.

From some of the comments John made, it may be speculated that he, as a soldier in Vietnam, had begun to exchange his traditional value system for a peer-oriented one. Since he was living with his peer group, there was no major struggle or upsetting conflict involved in gaining independence from old values. Although John's transnomic phase created no major emotional condition, his new values had not yet settled enough to have stabilized, and the old values were partially reawakened under parental reinforcement when John returned to the United States. While already functioning with a somewhat destabilized value system, this veteran was then, in addition, confronted with an existentially overwhelming antinomy. The timing of the antinomy impact was most unfortunate.

Polynomia is not part of John's condition. There was little or no investment in the values encountered through the contact with people from different cultures, classes, or religions, except for a few that were absorbed as peer values and played a role in the transnomic change.

John's condition can be summarized as follows: While involved in the transnomic phase between the tradition-directed and the peer-oriented stages of his moral development, John got involved in a severe case of antinomia with an anomic outcome.

RECOMMENDATIONS

The case discussed and its outcome illustrate clearly that a client can get lost in the no-man's-land between the territory claimed by the clergy and that occupied by the mental health professional. It also shows that withholding the help requested and needed can lead to serious consequences, which cannot be bypassed in terms of professional responsibility by invoking a territorial disclaimer.

The following recommendations are made in the hope that future clients can be served no matter what their problem is. The implementation of these recommendations will eliminate the value no-man's-land.

1. Closer ties need to be established between religious helping professionals and secular mental health professionals.
2. The field of values should not be viewed as the sole province of the religious professional. Inasmuch as values, and in particular transgressions against accepted values, can cause emotional problems, the field of social and moral values should be promoted as a field of mutual interest, rather than being one of bilateral abandonment.
3. Psychological and psychiatric research should be stepped up to map out the value field and to identify strategies of effective therapeutic intervention for value problems and in major value crises.
4. Training for mental health professionals should include courses in value theory and applicable treatment procedures as well as practica in which appropriate techniques are used in the treatment of the patient with problems stemming from the realm of values.
5. The clergy should be better equipped to deal with value issues beyond value teaching. The religious professionals need more information on the psychological implications of value theory, moral development, value transgressions, and so forth; and their education should involve training in effective dealing with value problems, especially when they are mental health related and require therapeutically constructive handling. And finally, the clergy should be made to understand more keenly their role as a moral reference authority and the psychological significance of that issue for a religiously oriented person's moral development.
6. In the interim, until both professional groups have caught up with training their members in effectively dealing with value problems, a list of professionals should be made available on the national level, in order to identify those individuals who are currently able to and interested in dealing with value issues. Only professionals should be listed who offer a nonbiased and nonproselytizing approach to values. Or if professionals are included who wish to promote a specific value system, as may be the case with some members of the clergy, then the value framework within which they operate should be clearly stated (such as, "value system: Baptist").

Obviously the most optimistic projection anticipates that in the future professionals from both camps will cooperate closely in helping people with value-related problems. And even if, once educated in the value field and its therapeutics, the two groups of professionals were to compete with each other rather than to cooperate, the clients would still be better off than they are now. Instead of getting no help, as can happen now, clients in the future are expected to get help cooperatively or competitively from *both* professionals: from the caretaker of the psyche and from the caretaker of the soul.

REFERENCES

Haley, S.A. (1978). Treatment implications of post-combat stress response syndromes for mental health professionals. In C. Figley (Ed.), *Stress disorders among Vietnam veterans.* (pp. 254-267). New York: Brunner/Mazel.

Lifton, J.R. (1978). Advocacy and corruption in the healing profession. In C. Figley, (Ed.), *Stress disorders among Vietnam veterans* (pp. 209-230). New York: Brunner/Mazel.

Ryan, W. (1971). *Blaming the victim.* New York: Random House.

Wick, E. (1983). *A new model of moral development.* (Unpublished manuscript.)

Assessing Religious Maturity

H. Newton Malony

I sometimes laughingly say, "I spent 4 years of my life in mental hospitals." And that is the truth. For 2 years I was a mental hospital chaplain and for 2 years I was a mental hospital psychologist.

In the hospital where I was chaplain I use to attend staff meetings and sit in a chair outside the "big table" around which sat the social workers, the psychiatrists, the psychologists and the psychiatric nurses. They were considered to be the REAL mental health professionals. The chaplain was not included in their deliberations and the most that was ever made of religion was when one of the psychiatrists would report, "I had the patient repeat 'Methodist Episcopal'"—as a gross index of brain damage in the mental-status examination. Occasionally a social worker would report that the patient was a "Baptist housewife" in giving the social history. But this was as much concern as was ever expressed about religion. The chaplain was never asked, "What is your religious diagnosis of the patient?"

Interestingly enough, things were different in the hospital where I was a psychologist. Here the chaplain sat around the table with the rest of us. In this hospital the chaplain was asked to make a report. The chaplain was part of the deliberations. The chief of chaplains at this hospital had constructed a rating scale for the chaplains to use in making their assessments. The scale helped the chaplains make judgments about how patients related to God, to themselves, and to others. In using the rating scale, the chaplain would ask patients questions about their religious faith and rate the answers as to whether they reflected a "defensive" or a "coping" use of religion.

Defensive religion was thought to be that which may have made patients feel better but which perpetuated their illness. It relieved symptoms but kept patients from self-awareness and indulged their dependency on their symptoms.

Coping religion was that which made patients feel good at the same time that it facilitated their getting well. It made patients self-aware, in-

H. Newton Malony received his PhD in clinical psychology from George Peabody College in 1964. He is in the private practice of psychotherapy and is on the faculty of the Graduate School of Psychology at Fuller Theological Seminary in Pasadena, California.

terdependent with God, stronger in their desire to get well, and less content to rely on their symptoms for adjustment.

Although this rating scale was helpful to the chaplains in making their reports, it was a crude instrument that served as a rough guide at best. There were no standard questions to ask nor were there clear guidelines upon which to base judgments.

Charles Hall, the senior chaplain of Topeka State Hospital who had constructed this rating scale, knew its weakness and asked psychologist Paul Pruyser of the nearby Menninger Foundation to assist him in refining the instrument. It was out of his collaboration with Chaplain Hall and his interest in these matters that Pruyser (1976) later wrote *The Minister As Diagnostician.* This volume reasserted the importance of making "religious" assessments in both diagnosis and in treatment. He emphasized the centrality of beliefs and suggested a number of dimensions in terms of which evaluations could be made.

Pruyser's book became the basis for the construction of Nelson-Malony Religious Status Interview (1982)—a 1-hour interview schedule, which is intended to provide mental health professionals a means for assessing religious maturity with a rationale and accuracy similar to that with which they assess intelligence and personality. A survey of noteworthy pastoral theologians and psychologists of religion evidenced no extant scale for such evaluation. The interview's light dimensions, 31 subscales and 43 questions, were also submitted to these scholars for their critique.

UNDERLYING ASSUMPTIONS

Several assumptions underlie the Religious Status Interview. They are as follows:

The first assumption is that "religion" refers to substantive social reality rather than dynamic subjective motivation. This preference for assessing a person's adherence to religion as it is seen objectively in cultural realities, for example, in the *Christian* faith, as opposed to assessing a person's individual feelings or urges about a transcendent dimension to life, follows the distinction made by Berger (1974) between religion as it appears in society and religion as it is inferred in subjective experience. The Nelson-Malony interview evaluates religious answers to life's questions (i.e., substantive religion) as opposed to the asking of religious questions (i.e., dynamic religion).

Secondly, it is an interview schedule which evaluates the *Christian religion,* not religion in general. In his book, Pruyser noted that it was time for psychologists to begin to pay attention to the content of peoples' religion in addition to its style. By this he meant that we should consider *what* people believe, not just *how* they believe. Therefore the Nelson-Malony interview intends to assess maturity in Christian faith rather than faith in general. It deals with matters of creation, redemption, justification forgiveness, and salvation—all essential categories of the Christian religion. It does not attempt to measure the religious status of Hindus, Buddhists, Muslims, or humanists. It leaves to practitioners of those faiths the task of constructing their own measurement tools. It limits itself to a single religion because of the conviction that there is no such thing as religion-in-general; this assumption was stated previously. The content of beliefs is important; and the authors, being Christian, felt best equipped to make judgments about that which they knew best.

However, in the third place, the interview schedule attempts to assess the way these beliefs function in the life of the person being evaluated. The authors attempt to combine ''functional'' with ''substantive'' religion. Although this procedure focuses on what people believe (i.e., substance), it, nevertheless, is primarily concerned with how these beliefs are used or incorporated into daily life (i.e., their function). For example, belief in God's grace is less important than whether and how God's grace is experienced in daily living.

The fourth assumption underlying the Nelson-Malony interview is that what people *say* about their religion is the *sine qua non* or essence of their faith. This places a priority on the ability to talk about one's faith, and this bias is intentional. Thus, the evaluation is confounded with verbal ability; however, it is not unlike the assumption on which intelligence and personality tests have been constructed. On the Wechsler tests of intelligence one is as smart as one's ability to answer questions and define words. On the Rorschach Ink Blot and the Thematic Apperception tests of personality, persons are judged on the basis of their ability to report perceptions verbally or to tell meaningful stories. Although many may seem hesitant to equate mature religion with verbal ability, the authors were convinced that being able to give religious rationales and interpretations for life events was the best estimate of this characteristic. Further, they assumed that thoughts precede action and that facility in verbal expressiveness is a central component of functional religion. It would seem that the Christian faith is primarily a unique interpretation of life that the believer understands or does not understand; and one's ability to explicitly apply that understanding and to self-consciously report it should be the optimal index of its presence or lack of it. Persons are no more religious, in this sense, than their ability to rationally relate the belief and their behavior.

The fifth assumption follows from the fourth. Here is it assumed that the ability to talk about religion should be spontaneous. Therefore, interviewers are encouraged to ask direct questions and to wait for the answers. While clarification of the question is appropriate, it is assumed that little effort should be put into trying to help persons express themselves or in pressuring them to speak when they seem hesitant. The rationale underlying this approach is that functional religion is that religion which functions automatically rather than that which functions under optimal or pressured conditions. It is thought that this is best measured by judging what people say when asked such questions as, "What does God mean to you?" without attempting to help them put their answers into more or better words. The habit or trait of being religious is, thus, more important to assess than the capacity to be religious.

Sixth, the interview is assumed to be both *reliable* and *valid*. At present these assumptions have been only partially supported. Studies, based on small samples, have found that it is possible for the same people to be interviewed by different interviewers and obtain similar responses. Further, it has been found that judges can independently score the same interviews similarly. Moreover, it has been concluded that persons will give similar responses to the questions when they are interviewed again 2 weeks later. Finally, when pastors were asked to nominate very mature, mature, and immature persons from their churches, their interview scores tended to correlate with designations by their pastor.

MATURITY DEFINED

Next, a definition of maturity was assumed. Based not only on Pruyser's *The Minister As Diagnostician* (1976), but also on Gordon Allport's *The Individual and His Religion* (1950/1961), Marie Jahoda's *Current Concepts of Positive Mental Health* (1958), and David Duncombe's *The Shape of the Christian Life* (1969), an understanding of mature Christian religion was divined. A statement of this understanding follows:

> Mature Christians are those who have identity, integrity, and inspiration. They "identify" in that their self-understanding is as children of God—created by Him and destined by Him to live according to a divine plan. They have "integrity" in that their daily life is lived in the awareness that they have been saved by God's grace from the guilt of sin and that they can freely respond to God's will in the present. They have "inspiration" in that they live with the sense that God is available to sustain, comfort, encourage, and direct their lives on a daily basis. These dimensions of maturity relate to belief in God the Father, God the Son, and God the Holy Spirit. They pertain to the Christian doctrines of creation, redemption, and sanctification. They provide the foundation for practical daily living.

Experientially, these beliefs result in a "freeing sense of security" which pervades the life of the mature Christian (Duncombe, 1969). In very practical and concrete ways Christian maturity results in very observable perceptions and very explicit behaviors. Duncombe's model is instructive for assuming that the Nelson-Malony interview model of maturity leads to optimal adjustment to life. It is shown in Table 1.

Here it can be seen that mature religion has effects which result in mature personality. It helps the person adjust to life in an effective and acceptable manner. The "freeing sense of security" which results in self-awareness, accurate perception, adequate expressiveness, and realistic interaction could be seen as an important and integral part of satisfying adjustment for any and all persons in any and all circumstances. Of course, like any state or trait in the person, this freeing sense of security exists along a continuum ranging from less to more. It is the presumption of the Nelson-Malony schedule that the more mature the religion, the greater will be this freeing sense of security.

This leads logically to the last assumption underlying this measure of religious maturity, namely, that the assessment of religious maturity can have an important place in the diagnosis and treatment of emotional problems. As noted earlier, this was the presumption of the staff at Topeka State Hospital when they included the chaplain in case conferences. Such an assessment could and, perhaps, should be a part of such decisions in all mental health facilities.

Religion is an important part of many, if not most, people's lives. This is certainly true in the United States where the vast majority report believing in a God and where organized religion is an obvious part of public life. Thus, religious faith is probably just as important to assess as ego strength, interpersonal relations, self-concept, and emotional control.

TABLE 1

THE RESULTS OF FAITH

"A FREEING SENSE OF SECURITY"

		INTERNAL RESULTS	EXTERNAL RESULTS
PASSIVE	MODALITY	SELF AWARENESS	ACCURATE PERCEPTION
ACTIVE	MODALITY	HONEST EXPRESSION	REALISTIC INTERACTION

(Adapted From D. Duncombe The Shape of The Christian Life. New York: Abingdon Press, 1969, p. 22)

RELIGIOUS MATURITY AND TREATMENT

As with all assessments, the measurement of religious maturity has import for three types of decisions: diagnosis, general mental status, and treatment. *Diagnostic decisions* pertain to the question of causation. The central issue is, "What caused the person to have the problem they have?" In the case of religion, the issue is, "Whether and/or how does the person's religious faith provoke the person to become disturbed or emotionally upset?" *General mental status* refers to the person's basic personality and intellectual structure on top of which they became disturbed. The question here is, "What are the characteristics of the person's premorbid functioning?" In regard to religion, the issue is, "Is this person's religious faith a basic strength or an essential weakness of his or her personhood quite apart from the problem being experienced?". *Treatment* refers to the plan for effecting change. The question here is, "What should be the components of the treatment plan?" In the case of religion, the issue is, "Can this person's religious faith be used as a resource to call on in working with this person or will it be a weakness to be overcome or ignored?"

In regard to diagnosis, it should be obvious that variations in level of religious maturity might make religion more a cause of emotional disturbance in certain situations. In regard to general mental status, having a religious faith that was judged to be a personality strength might prove to be an asset in preventing mental illness from becoming worse. Finally, in regard to treatment, it is important to know whether one can utilize a person's religious faith in the intervention process. Making these judgments about religious maturity is potentially valuable addenda to almost all clinical decisions in the mental health professions.

DIMENSIONS ASSESSED

One would be hard pressed to find treatment goals more encompassing than those mentioned by Duncombe (1969). His conviction that religion can enhance or impede self-awareness, accurate perception, adequate expressiveness, and realistic interaction is fundamental to the Nelson-Malony interview.

Turning to the content of the Nelson-Malony Religious Status Interview, there are eight dimensions which are assessed. These are (1) Awareness of God, (2) Acceptance of God's Grace and Steadfast Love, (3) Being Repentant and Responsible, (4) Knowing God's Leadership and Direction, (5) Involvement in Organized Religion, (6) Experiencing Fellowship, (7) Being Ethical, and (8) Affirming Openness in Faith. A person can be judged mature in one or more dimensions and thus be more or less balanced in maturity or immaturity. However, the major interest is in an overall or general measure of maturity across all dimensions.

Definitions of maturity in each of the eight dimensions are as follows:

Awareness of God. Mature persons stand in awe before God as creatures and are aware of their Creator. Mature persons express awareness of their dependence upon the Creator, but also recognize their capabilities. Mature persons show humility in the face of life's besetting problems and have a realistic awareness of their own creaturely limitations but do not deny their own capacity for productive action. Mature persons worship God as an expression of reverence and of love toward God. Mature persons pray as a means of spiritual sustenance and communion with God and as a way of honestly expressing concerns.

Acceptance of God's grace and steadfast love. Mature persons view God as loving them unconditionally. Mature persons use God's love and forgiveness as an impetus for new life and responsible action. Mature persons appreciate God's love and manifest this through a sense of joy and gratitude. Mature persons have the ability to find meaning in the suffering and difficulties of life. This meaning is based on trust in God and His goodness.

Being repentant and responsible. Mature persons accurately accept personal responsibility without denying other factors, such as the environment, in personal difficulties and in sin. Mature persons' attitudes toward repentance are based on constructive sorrow which leads to a concern to correct the situation. Mature persons are aware of their inner impulses and accept them as a legitimate part of their humanness. Mature persons are able to request and to accept forgiveness from others without feeling threatened or self-depreciating. Mature persons are forgiving of others without experiencing continued resentment toward them.

Knowing God's leadership and direction. Mature persons express trust in God's leadership for life yet also recognize their role in that process. Mature persons express an optimistic, yet realistic, hope based on trust in God. Without denying present problems, mature persons are confident that God is in control of life. Mature persons have a positive sense of role identity that provides meaning in relation to faith.

Involvement in organized religion. Mature persons experience regular weekly involvement with others in religious worship, prayer, study, and service. Mature persons evidence active involvement and commitment to religious activities. Mature persons are involved in church or in a religious group as an index of their desire to grow in their faith.

Experiencing fellowship. Mature persons experience relationships at various levels of intimacy including interdependent, growth-oriented relationships with other believers. Mature persons identify positively with the family of God and have a sense of community with other believing persons as well as with people everywhere. Mature persons have a sense of commonality with all of God's creatures and with God's creation.

Being ethical. Mature persons follow their ethical principles in a flexible but committed manner. Mature persons' religious faith strongly underlies and guides their ethical behavior. Mature persons show a concern for personal and social ethics. Their acts evidence that they have a concern for both and are concerned about individual responsibility and social justice. Mature persons have a sense that they are serving others through their work or vocation.

Affirming openness in faith. Mature persons' faith provides a directive for life as a whole. Mature persons spend a significant time reading about their faith and discussing it with others as an expression of a desire to grow in faith. While expressing confidence in their own view, mature persons show a tolerance for other viewpoints and evidence a willingness to examine others' beliefs in an honest manner. Mature persons' faith is differentiated and is composed of a relatively large number of categories and elements.

Taken together, it is the conviction of the authors that these dimensions are an adequate measure of religious maturity from the viewpoint of the Jewish/Christian faith. They are indices of how mature faith can function in life to assure accurate self and other perceptions coupled with adequate expression and action.

CONCLUSION

This essay has described a relatively new systematic attempt to assess religious maturity. It is not the first or only such attempt. As early as 1965, Draper, Meyer, Parzen, and Samuelson reported an attempt to assess the diagnostic value of religious ideation in response to a Group for the Advancement of Psychiatry report calling for such investigation. However, Draper and his colleagues seemed more preoccupied with using religious ideas to categorize patients' types of emotional disturbance than with assessing mature faith. The Nelson-Malony Religious Status Interview (1982), described herein, is an attempt to remedy this lack of attention to mature religion.

It is felt that the Nelson-Malony Religious Status Interview provides a means whereby mental health professionals may make valid and reliable judgments about the degree to which the functional Christian faith of their clients/patients is contributing to their disturbance, their mental state, and their potential response to treatment.

It is felt that the underlying assumptions accord with Feinsilver's (1960) 3-R test for religious maturity in spite of the fact that the Nelson-

Malony assumptions pertain explicitly to the Christian faith and not to religion in general. The Christianity of the Religious Status Interview, discussed herein, is indeed reasonable (it comes to terms with modern thought); responsible (it generates social concern); and related (it connects persons to others and to the physical world).

Furthermore, the underlying assumptions also accord well with Orlo Strunk's 15 questions about mature religion in his 1965 book.

Thus, there is now available a means for assessing religious maturity through the interview medium. Only the future will tell how valuable such an evaluation can be. Although unaccustomed to making such judgments, mental health professionals may come to agree with Anton Boisen, the founder of clinical pastoral education, who reportedly said that knowing about a person's religion was the most important knowledge a counselor could have.

REFERENCES

Allport, G. (1961). *The individual and his religion.* New York: Macmillan. (Originally published 1950.)

Berger, P.L. (1974). Second thoughts on defining religion. *The Journal for the Scientific Study of Religion, 13,* 125-133.

Draper, E., Meyer, G.G., Parzen, Z., & Samuelson, G. (1965). On the diagnostic value of religious ideation. *Archives of General Psychiatry, 13,* 202-207.

Duncombe, D.C. (1969). *The stages of the Christian life.* New York: Abingdon Press.

Feinsilver, M. (1960). *In search of religious maturity.* Yellow Springs, OH: Antioch Press.

Jahoda, M. (1958). *Current concepts of positive mental health.* New York: Basic Books.

Nelson, D.O. & Malony, H.N. (1982). *The religious status interview.* Unpublished document, Fuller Theological Seminary, Pasadena, CA.

Pruyser, P. (1976). *The minister as diagnostician.* Philadelphia, PA: Westminster Press.

Strunk, O. (1965). *Mature religion: A psychological study.* New York: Abingdon Press.

The Religious Patient's Initial Encounter with Psychotherapy

Carole A. Rayburn

INTRODUCTION

Religion and psychology have not always been viewed as allies by their adherents, though there seems to be some narrowing of the significant gaps between pastoral counseling and psychotherapy as they are traditionally practiced. Nonetheless, there is still a chasm in the philosophical handling of religious material in psychotherapeutic intervention. Some have argued against justifying values by reference to supernatural authority, warning of the possible danger of integrating religious values into psychotherapy (Walls, 1980). Others have argued that it is impossible to have a value-free psychotherapy (Bergin, 1980a, b; Barron, 1973; R. Cox, 1973; and Rayburn, in press-a). Bergin has further insisted that, in the growing public and professional interest in religious values and issues, religion should take a central rather than a peripheral place in clinical psychology. Certainly the shifts from a questioning of the relevance of religious values in the modern world (H. Cox, 1966) to a view stressing the vitality of religion in the current world of politics and in other arenas (H. Cox, 1984) has been well documented. Cox, in fact, suggests that ultimately a social religious consciousness will prevail in our world.

Some have perceived possible common grounds between pastoral counseling and psychotherapy, with the holistic nature of individuals being considered in the totality of body, mind, and spirit (Rayburn, 1983). However, many disagree on some of the emphases given to religious material in psychotherapy. Bergin, for instance, sees guilt as an important protector for the individual's psyche and for society, and he insists that conscience not be dismissed as an outmoded set of controls but be an in-

Dr. Carole A. Rayburn received her PhD from The Catholic University of America and her MDiv. from Andrews University Seventh-day Adventist Theological Seminary. She is a clinical and consulting psychologist in Silver Spring, Maryland. Dr. Rayburn is president of the Maryland Psychological Association and president of the Section on the Clinical Psychology of Women of the American Psychological Association's Division of Clinical Psychology.

tegral part of a functioning human being. Walls, however, thinks that Bergin's urging that values take a central position in psychotherapy may lead to therapists not critically assessing their values and not submitting them to rational scrutiny. Smudski (1976) has commented on religion being psychologized as a response to the crisis of belief in our society, with frustration sometimes leading to lessening of religious beliefs.

THE RELIGIOUSLY COMMITTED PATIENT

Some Studies of Religious Populations

In studies of religious individuals and their personality traits, there has not always been adequate control for social class differences among the various religious denominations. However, religious students have been found to be more anxious, to feel less adequate, and to have lower self-esteem than nonreligious students (Dittes, 1969; Lea, 1982); religious individuals have been found to be more defensive and dependent (Dreger, 1952), to complain more often of tension (Rokeach, 1960), to be less self-actualizing and less self-accepting (Graff & Ladd, 1971; Hjelle, 1975; Maslow, 1962). Overall, little evidence has been found that religion per se either causes or prevents emotional disturbance.

Lovinger (1979) pointed out some cultural differences among Catholics (whom he saw as severely and rigidly moralistic with a very punitive superego) and among Jews (with problems of independence and dependence concerning their families, especially their mothers; self-assertion; ambivalent relations and attitudes concerning out-group members; and introversion and overeating).

Pastoral Counseling with the Religiously Committed

Before they ever consider being seen by a psychotherapist, the religiously committed individuals may have sought help from pastoral counselors. Ostow and Cholst (1974) note that often those suffering distress from family problems turn to clergy and other pastoral counselors first, usually rejecting the possibility that such discord could be related to emotional disturbance. In many such instances, these persons want the counselor to influence the behavior of the significant others in their lives. If they are depressed and seeking a rescue from hopelessness and helplessness, they may see clergypersons as God's representatives and as omnipotent parent symbols who might be willing to denounce or otherwise humiliate spouses whom they accuse of being disloyal. They may use their interpretations of biblical injunctions to get clergy to do their bidding with others (e.g., "Shouldn't my husband/wife place my happiness above the interests of parents?").

Virkler (1979) discussed the felt inadequacies of pastors in handling sexual counseling, depression, feelings of inadequacy, and vocational counseling. He suggested that there is a need to study further the whole idea of pastors' attitudes toward sexuality. Further, he hypothesized that the reason that sexual problems are rarely brought to pastors may be due to explicit or implicit messages that pastors send out concerning sexuality. Hennessy and Varga (1975) discussed the specific need for religious counselors to be nonjudgmental of their clients. They saw the need for such counselors to be not only extremely accepting of those seeking help but also to be genuine, aware of their own frailties, and displaying the greatest degree of forgiveness.

Religiously Committed Patients and Their Initial Encounter with Therapy

When religiously committed patients do come for psychotherapy, they have a preference for treatment from religious psychotherapists. This is especially true in the case of psychotherapists whose religious beliefs are congruent with those of the prospective patients. Doughtery and Worthington (1982) have suggested that such congruence between patient and therapist beliefs about religious values is a stronger determinant for preferred treatment than are psychological factors such as emphasis on insight versus behavior.

The religious individual may have a set of irrational beliefs about psychology, psychologists and psychiatrists, and psychotherapy, with the intensity of the distortion varying from denomination to denomination and within different geographical locations and type of setting (academic campuses and the environs versus rural settings, for example). Psychotherapy may even be seen as the ''brainwashing tool'' of secular high priests. This was dramatically shown to me on the day when I was baptized into a more fundamental Protestant denomination, after having been a long-standing member of a mainstream Protestant group. Two women commented spontaneously and joyfully, ''Imagine it: How wonderful that you are a psychologist *and* a believer! We didn't think that anyone could be both!''. So I had achieved some presumed salvation from the ''darkness'' of psychology! I was now saved!

Not long after joining the church, however, I was constantly sought after each week after church service. Several members practically formed a line to speak to me about their spiritual and psychological problems. Since I thought it would be more appropriate to refer them to another therapist and certainly to someone whom they could see during the week, I was somewhat surprised that this offer met with massive resistance. I was quickly told that they did not approve of psychotherapy because it could be ''satanic'' and because, to yield to going to a therapist ''would be showing distrust in God and not having enough faith in my prayer life.'' When I respectfully reminded them that I was both a psychologist and a psychotherapist, and that if they confided their problems to me they could also do this with another therapist, they insisted, "No, it is different telling you, because you are one of us and we are telling you in church.''

Fortunately for my professional practice, I was able to transcend such a narrow attitude with religious people, though in another setting. Strangely, it was when I left my large suburban area and the site of the world headquarters of my denomination for the tiny college town of my seminary in the midwest that I began to see those of my faith in psychotherapy in abundance. Probably this was for several reasons: Most of the composition of the college town in which the seminary was situated was made up of those of my faith; I was now "kosher," having seminary training as well as psychology training; and I had the blessings—and referrals—from the pastoral counseling leaders in the community to conduct the psychotherapy with these individuals.

Many of those whom I saw in therapy during my seminary days were experiencing marital problems. They typically had married very early, at least by the time they were 17 or 18 years old. Often this was due to a misunderstanding of the religious teachings or of sexual behavior, with their parents enforcing an extremely rigid moral code upon them when the young couple had been found to be petting or necking and this was held up to them as comparable to having had sexual intercourse and thus necessitated (in the minds of the parents) marriage as soon as possible. Then, at the age of 30-35, they look across the table from each other, often incompatible strangers who need to restore the fervor to their relationship. Such individuals must overcome some sense of shame and a felt loss of status when they seek help through psychotherapy. Some may be leaders within the religious community, or else they may come from well-known families within the religious establishment. They may have enjoyed prestigious positions as role models for those new to the faith, and coming for psychotherapy represents falling off an honored pedestal of success. Often they begin to doubt the sincerity and intensity of their belief in divine authority, and then they doubt themselves and may become intropunitive and obsessive-compulsive.

It is imperative for the therapist to listen to the patient with sensitivity and from as nonjudgmental a perspective as possible. Religious patients more than any other kind of patients are apt to experience their problems as felt punishment for some sin and to sense varying degrees of guilt for the misdeed. Traditionally, psychotherapy has tended to make light of or to deny any guilt feelings present in patients or to admit that the guilt is there but should be nullified as soon as possible. No matter how uncomfortable the therapist is with such reflections on guilt, the patient who is religious must deal with this as part of her or his world of reality. While helping the patient to look critically at any irrational thinking going on and aiming to understand any feelings present is vital, the therapist of religious persons will emerge less than authentic if real felt guilt and hopefully forgiveness of the self and others is invalidated because of therapist discomfort in dealing directly with such issues.

Here it is important to encourage patients to develop a more realistic conception of perfection. Their striving to attain nothing less than a perfection of self on this earth can often lead to depression, despondency, and even suicidal ideation. A young man whom I treated while at seminary was convinced that, because he did not seem called to the gospel ministry, he should be a perfect colporteur and sell a tremendous volume of religious literature every month. The goals that he set for himself were so high that he was bound to fail in his efforts to achieve this kind of perfection. He was ruining his life, his marriage, and his job satisfaction. Not succeeding in this enterprise, he succumbed to obsessive-compulsive behavior at which he could gain control: He would stop his car en route to his sales territory each day to pick up sticks, branches, rocks, and other obstacles in his path on the road. This delayed him from spending that much more time on the job toward which he held ambivalent feelings. Even here, he did not want to own the counterproductive behavior as something that he was doing to deal with his problems. A martyr to the end, he convinced himself that he was nobly clearing the path for other motorists. Such patients need to be shown that no one occupational skill or personality attribute defines their self-worth or self-actualizing. They need to be helped to more clearly define for themselves their immediate and long-term goals. Perfection should be seen more on a continuum toward which one is continually striving but at which one does not arrive suddenly nor usually early in life.

It might well be pointed out to the perfectionistic, rigid religious person that such a bent is often fostered by narcissism rather than by any true desire to sacrifice for the benefit of others. In suffering en route to perfection—and usually the suffering is somewhat less than silent—attention is drawn to the self and not to the cause for which one is supposedly enduring pain or for the divine authority one wishes to heed. There usually are control issues involved, plus some irrational thinking, such as, "If I am perfect or almost perfect, everyone else should also be perfect." Suspiciousness may arise here, too: "I had better make sure that everyone is acting in such a way to become (remain) perfect, and while I am checking on how perfect they are I will detract their attention from looking to see how perfect I am." The syndrome for "looking over my shoulders at the sinners" may thus be set up in the untreated religious perfectionist. It would be well to point out to religious patients that scriptural perfection means "complete" or "finished," the attainment of the end of being. Only the divine has absolute perfection, and so Matthew 5:48 ("You,

therefore must be perfect, as your heavenly Father is perfect'') is comple-
mented by I John 1:8 ("If we say we have no sin, we deceive ourselves,
and the truth is not in us") and Philippians 3:12 ("Not that I have already
obtained this or am already perfect; but I press on to make it my own, because Christ Jesus has made me his own").

Religiously committed patients, in their initial encounter with psychotherapy, then, might have several fears. They may fear never being
whole, sensing a fragmentation of not being a totality. As a defense
against such a fear, the individual may try to transcend the situation to
find answers of life and to gain control in the search for a cure to the fragmentation (R. Cox, 1973). Besides fearing that receiving psychotherapeutic treatment means a slacking of one's prayer life and a decrease in
faith in God, religious persons may fear being misunderstood and criti-
cized for their belief in religious matters, being encouraged to renounce
and/or make light of their religious convictions in favor of more worldly
values, and fear expressing the "darker sides of their natures." It is beneficial to note to such patients that there are some strong parallels between
religion and psychology, such as the "confession" of religion and the
"catharsis" of psychotherapy, both stressing the release of powerful
emotions in an effort to purge the individual of devastating feelings (Rayburn, 1983).

Beit-Hallahmi (1975), discussing the problems of the irreligious therapist working with the religious patient, emphasizes the cognitive problem
of knowing and understanding the meaning of specific religious behaviors
and beliefs. There is also the therapeutic problem of dealing with the pa-
tient-therapist gap in beliefs. Therapists need to give sufficient credit to
the importance of religious values in the life of religious patients. Therapists need to be continually aware of their imposing personalities and
positions of authority in even the religious patient's world. When they attempt to be more honest and open with patients through self-disclosure of
their own religious or spiritual beliefs, therapists may be less than percep-
tive and honest in admitting differences with patients' value systems
and/or they may challenge the patients' beliefs. Occasionally the religious
patient needs to establish a boundary between himself or herself and the
therapist by demanding to know the position of the therapist regarding
religious values. The therapist does well to assure the patient that though
the same beliefs may not be shared in common, this will not impede their
working together on other problems.

Lovinger (1979) also discussed problems of countertransference in
working with religious patients, as well as the therapist's reluctance in
dealing with value systems, the often-sensed lack of effective therapeutic
strategies, and difficulties in handling biblical literature. On one occasion, the elderly parents of a 35-year-old woman addicted to drugs and
severely depressed came in for the initial psychotherapy session to inter-

view me and to discern my religious convictions. They requested such a session quite openly, stating that their daughter was refusing to see a therapist and that they wanted to have an appropriate therapist who was willing to see her, once she was ready for treatment. While I would be opposed to selection of a patient whom I would treat based on merely seeing her parents (whose intervention might have proven to be detrimental to overall treatment, if continuous and obstructionistic), sometimes an exception may be made in the interest of assuring pained families that respect for their beliefs will be maintained. Of course, this is said with the understanding that such beliefs are not held to be counterproductive to the overall progress of the patient. Usually, though, it is not so much the beliefs per se but distortions of the beliefs which adversely affect the emotional health of persons.

Strunk (1965) has suggested a way in which to discern what a mature religious belief is. He considers a belief mature when it may be seen in behavior demonstrating the fostering of social concern and involvement in one's environment (there is contact with society rather than withdrawal and solitude); intellectual and spiritual awareness forming the basis of such beliefs; personal conviction of the existence of a transcendental power greater than oneself; and not compartmentalizing religion by cutting it off from other aspects of life in the larger world. Feinsilver (1960) also sees the test of a responsible religious belief system as religion which generates social concern, not only "comforting the afflicted" but "afflicting the comfortable."

Besides seeking to avoid being rejected or ridiculed by their therapists, religiously committed patients may specifically need support and confirmation from the therapist (who may then be serving as a nurturing parent surrogate). The importance of the religious belief structure in the religious person's life must not be underestimated or seen as psychologically irrelevant to the patient. Religious issues must be considered both from the dynamic context of the religious and the personal. In addition to being determinants of the patient's identity, such values and beliefs may show the beginning of the breaking away from parental influences and the inception of independent and separate life-styles. Gaps in the religious beliefs of therapist and patient make it necessary to recognize differences and similarities openly and honestly and without creating a lot of tension.

The areas of assertiveness and of anger often present special problems to religious patients, particularly to the novice of psychotherapy intervention. Russell (1983) pointed out that some Christians may feel uneasy about assertiveness because they confuse assertion with aggression, and they also may see nonassertive behavior as synonymous with Christian behavior. The cognitive barrier of the patient's belief that Christ's interpersonal life-style is opposed to an assertive approach needs to be explored and confronted; many instances may be shown to substantiate that this is not so (Romans 1:18, Mark 3:5, 11:15, for instance). To the less religious therapist, such an appeal to biblical evidence and reasoning may appear inappropriate or even unethical (since the particular therapist may not feel qualified to address these issues in that manner). Such therapists may, however, still feel comfortable enough with the appeal to both spiritual and emotional health of "do not let the sun go down on your anger," the idea of Matthew 5:21-24 of expressing the anger constructively and coming to a reconciliation and forgiveness with others. The wholeness possible in relating to others in an empathic, assertive way and seeking to communicate openly, honestly, respectfully, and lovingly is not only consistent with biblical literature but in agreement with the best teachings of emotional well-being.

Hower (1974) suggested that human anger is about the same as God's anger, a reaction to violations of one's personal system of righteousness ("how things ought to be"). Human anger is difficult to understand and deal with because the indignation is sometimes distorted and individualized, erroneous expressions of anger may be proffered (e.g., vengeance), and there may be an unwillingness to accept responsibility of disciplining others in kindness through giving them the necessary angry feedback which can result in repentance. Anger can best be handled in psychotherapy with religious patients, Hower thinks, through the use of introspection, reflection, insight, rearrangement of presuppositions, and giving feedback to the offender.

Among some religious patients, even those relatively happy in their religious convictions, there is sometimes a sense of loneliness and isolation from the larger world outside the religious in-group constellation. In my clinical practice, I saw such lonely and saddened religious patients who primarily were members of the more fundamentalist and cultic groups. A couple from such a denomination traveled hundreds of miles for their therapy sessions, not wanting to be treated in the small town in which they lived. The husband was a politician who, in order to keep in touch with his constituents, often went into restaurants with bars to greet them. His religious beliefs not only opposed drinking alcohol (which he was not doing) but traditionally encouraged the avoidance or shunning of such places as bars, dance halls, and movies. Further, his religious group, through its traditions and mores, looked down upon any of its members pursuing a political career. Once, however, he had set about on this course of endeavor, he was experiencing ambivalence, confusion, and isolation because of the dissonance between his religious and his professional beliefs. An affable person, he wanted to share his philosophies of life with those from all backgrounds. His wife, a firm believer in the separation of those of their religion from those outside of the denomination, had strong feelings against what her husband was doing. She wanted him to limit his contacts to those within their faith. This disagreement had reached such proportions that she was considering leaving him. Discussions with them about sharing their faith and philosophy with those outside their own immediate group, an appeal to the wife that those within her own group might be in less need of such sharing than those outside it, and the use of Mark 9:50 which concerns going out among all kinds of people in our society (as did the Christian model Jesus) were very helpful in getting them back together again.

A growing group of religious, isolated individuals who may be coming for psychotherapy in increasing numbers from now on are the religious feminists. These are the women and men who, while often satisfied with the basic theological teachings of their religions, are quite disheartened with the lack of social awareness or concern of the religion as it is lived. The religious feminists witness countless instances of gender and racial discrimination, as well as class elitism. They develop severe cases of ambivalence, confusion, shock reaction, loneliness, and a sense of loss in the battle within themselves and between themselves and their religion, as well as between the religious establishment and the rest of society. Such persons desperately want to hold onto their faith and to their belief in the equality of all people. The women in such groups need to find their womanhood and their personhood, independent from the inhibiting traditional ways of a nonegalitarian world (Rayburn, 1981a, 1981b, 1982; Rayburn, Natale, & Linzer, 1982). Many feel as though they are doomed to be spiritual nomads, wandering between the religious and the feminist worlds and being urged by each group to give up membership in the other group.

Not happy at the thought of leaving either group, though, they continue their struggles and are constantly under much stress. When they initially come for psychotherapy, they need reassurance that it is all right to seek dual membership in the two worlds. They need to know that going against parent messages of their religious traditions and not turning their backs on those who seek acceptance within their sanctuary walls—the women, minorities, and poor as well as the generally more accepted white, affluent, males—is accepted by society at large, represented here by the therapist.

Therapists treating religious feminists may be tempted to take sides with or against the religious establishment. That, however, would be a grave mistake. These patients need to work out such problems for themselves, carefully and critically, in the backdrop of a caring, nonjudgmental, and unconditionally accepting environment with the therapist. Therapists need to be well rounded in the psychology of women; the need to use nonsexist language; the recognition of the negative impact of sexist language—especially language of God and faith—on many religious women (who do not care for what seems noninclusive language which walls women out of the mainstream of interaction with others in religious settings [Rayburn, in press-b]); and the acceptance of guidelines such as those published by the Division of Counseling Psychology of the American Psychological Association, for working with women in counseling and psychotherapy. Therapists need to look beyond tradition, of religion and of society in general, in helping the religious feminist to find new options to old and new problems and to develop realistic hope and inspiration on the way to true self-actualization.

A word of caution for the therapist working with novices in religious feminism: be patient, listen, explore, and do not push or cubbyhole the patients into any corners. Allow them to work through the incongruences in their lives in an accepting and warm atmosphere. Working with them on the most effective and realistic ways to approach their problems is highly beneficial, particularly with an appreciation of the two spheres of interest encompassing their being. They need uncritical, caring, nurturing concern in which to grow and survive through the duality of their seeking. Affirm and applaud their bravery in such a tedious search for truth. Deal openly with their many pains and frustrations, and with the seriousness of their plight.

Therapists working with religiously committed patients, whether the therapists are religious or nonreligious (or, as some prefer to be seen, "spiritual, but not religious"), have many decided challenges before them. They are cognitive barriers of biblical and other religious literature, different language and concepts, and various traditions of religious groups which at times may seem even more differentiating than differences in cultures and nationalities. Those from religious groups, as other persons and sometimes even more so, need special understanding, acceptance, and help. They may not behave as most people who are not as religious behave, and this is especially true the more fundamentalist or cultic their beliefs. However, the therapist will find great rewards in a job well done with the religious.

REFERENCES

Barron, J. (1973). The psychotherapist as priest, prophet, holy man, "religious" educator, and person. In R. Cox (Ed.), *Religious systems and psychotherapy*. Springfield, IL: Charles C. Thomas.

Beit-Hallahmi, B. (1975). Encountering orthodox religion in psychotherapy. *Psychotherapy: Theory, Research, and Practice, 12*(4), 357-359.

Bergin, A.E. (1980a). Psychotherapy and religious values. *Journal of Consulting and Clinical Psychology. 48*(1), 95-105.

Bergin, A.E. (1980b). Religious and humanistic values: A reply to Ellis and Walls. *Journal of Consulting and Clinical Psychology, 48*(5), 642-645.

Cox, H. (1966). *The secular city.* New York: Macmillan.

Cox, H. (1984). *After the secular city: Religion and politics in the post-modern world.* New York: Simon & Schuster.

Cox, R. (1973). An introduction to human guidance. In R. Cox (Ed.), *Religious systems and psychotherapy.* Springfield, IL: Charles C. Thomas.

Dittes, J.E. (1969). Psychology of religion. In G. Lindzey & E. Aronson (Eds.), *The handbook of social psychology.* Reading, MA: Addison-Wesley.

Doughtery, S.G., & Worthington, E.L. (1982). Preferences of conservative and moderate Christians for four Christian counselors' treatment plans. *Journal of Psychology and Theology, 10*(4), 346-354.

Dreger, R.M. (1952). Some personality correlates of religious attitudes as determined by projective techniques. *Psychology Monographs, 66*(3).

Feinsilver, A. (1960). *In search of religious maturity.* Yellow Springs, OH: Antioch Press.

Graff, R.W., & Ladd, C.E. (1971). POI (Personality Orientation Inventory) correlates of a religious commitment inventory. *Journal of Clinical Psychology, 27,* 502-504.

Hennessy, T.C., & Varga, A.C. (1975). A religious perspective on sexual counseling. *Counseling Psychologist, 5*(1), 111-114.

Hjelle, L. (1975). Relationship of a measure of self-actualization to religious participation. *Journal of Psychology, 89,* 179-182.

Hower, J.T. (1974). The misunderstanding and mishandling of anger. *Journal of Psychology and Theology, 2*(4), 269-275.

Lea, G. (1982). Religion, mental health, and clinical issues. *Journal of Religion and Health, 21*(4), 336-351.

Lovinger, R.J. (1979). Therapeutic strategies with religious resistances. *Psychotherapy: Theory, Research, and Practice, 16*(4), 419-427.

Maslow, A.H. (1962). *Toward a psychology of being.* Princeton, NJ: Van Nostrand.

Ostow, M., & Cholst, B. (1974). Unhappiness and mental health. *New York State Journal of Medicine, 74*(6), 984-992.

Rayburn, C.A. (1981a). Some reflections of a female seminarian: Woman, whither goest thou? *Journal of Pastoral Counseling, 16*(2), 61-65.

Rayburn, C.A. (1981b). Wilderness wanderings. In E. M. Stern (Ed.), *The other side of the couch: What therapists believe.* New York: Pilgrim Press.

Rayburn, C.A. (1982). Seventh-day Adventist women: Values, conflicts, and resolutions. *Journal of Pastoral Counseling, 17*(1), 19-22.

Rayburn, C.A. (in press-a). Impact of nonsexist language and guidelines for women in religion. *Journal of Pastoral Counseling.*

Rayburn, C.A. (in press-b). Some comparisons of religion with psychology and psychotherapy. *Journal of Pastoral Counseling.*

Rayburn, C.A., Natale, S.M., & Linzer, J. (1982). Faminism and religion: What price holding membership in both camps? *Counseling and Values, 27*(2), 83-89.

Rokeach, M. (1960). *The open and closed mind.* New York: Basic Books.

Russell, R.A. (1983). Cognitive barriers to assertiveness for the Christian. *Counseling and Values, 27*(2), 83-89.

Smudski, J.R. (1976). The crisis of belief and the psychologizing of religion. *Journal of Religion and Health, 15*(2), 94-99.

Strunk, O. (1965). *Mature religion: A psychological study.* New York: Abingdon Press.

Virkler, H.A. (1974). Counseling demands, procedures, and preparation of parish ministers: A descriptive study. *Journal of Psychology and Theology, 7*(4), 271-280.

Walls, G.B." (1980). Values and psychotherapy: A comment on "psychotherapy and religious values." *Journal of Consulting and Clinical Psychology, 48*(5), 640-641.

Forgiveness:
A Spiritual Psychotherapy

Kenneth Wapnick

In this article I am proposing a theoretical model for a spiritual approach to psychotherapy, based on the principles of an inspired set of three books called *A Course in Miracles* (1975) and its companion pamphlet: "Psychotherapy: Purpose, Practice, Process." The Course is unique in its integration of a profound metaphysical system with the basic principles of psychodynamic psychology, an integration that has direct practical implications for our everyday living as well as for psychotherapy. The first part of this article presents an outline of the basic principles of this model, while the second discusses their specific application to psychotherapy.

I

The theoretical framework of the Course rests on the contrast between two thought systems: God and the ego. Our true reality, created by God, is spirit. This is our real Self, which is formless, changeless, and eternal. The ego is the false self, which has its home in the body, and which changes, suffers, and dies. The ego's world is that of perception, the home of illusions and fear. It came into existence at the instant that the thought of separation entered into the mind of our real Self. This thought was the insane belief that it was possible to attack God, thereby establishing a will, self, and world separate and independent from the Will, Self, and Heaven that He created. From this thought arose the world of the body, which returns to the separated mind the witnesses that speak of what is inherently illusory, in contrast to the inherent truth of Heaven.

This is the underlying metaphysics upon which rests the more practical focus of the Course: how to live in this world of separation from God, and

---

Kenneth Wapnick received his PhD in clinical psychology from Adelphi University in 1968. He is presently in private practice in Crompond, New York, and is president of the Foundation for a Course in Miracles.

how to return to Him. On this level, the world is understood to be a class-room, where we come to learn the lessons that would ultimately teach us where our true Home is. The phenomenal world is not denied, but rein-terpreted to maximize our learning. As the Course (*A Course in Miracles: Manual for Teachers*, 1975) states: "It takes great learning to understand that all things, events, encounters, and circumstances are helpful. It is on-ly to the extent to which they are helpful that any degree of reality should be accorded them in this world of illusion (p. 9). In psychotherapy we have one of the most helpful tools to free people from the distorted ways of thinking and perceiving that prevent this return.

The central element in the ego's thought system is guilt, which be-comes the chief obstacle to remembering our real Self. Guilt rests on the belief that we have done terrible things and are, in fact, terrible people. Thus we may define guilt as encompassing all the negative beliefs, ex-periences, and concepts we have about ourselves, including feelings of in-adequacy, inferiority, worthlessness, and shame associated with our physical and psychological selves. Each of us is born guilty, the claims of modern-day Rousseauvians notwithstanding that children are innocent, angelic creatures, corrupted by a corrupt world. Freud's description of infants as polymorphous perverse seems closer to the truth. Indeed, Freud showed just how far back in our development these feelings of shame and inadequacy are manifest. It is beyond the scope of the present article to discuss the ultimate origins of this guilt, beyond stating that it rests on the fundamental belief that we have indeed separated ourselves from God.* Sufficient for our purpose is recognizing that guilt is an in-herent part of our experience in this world.

One of the more painful characteristics of guilt is its demand for pun-ishment. If I feel guilty over some perceived wrongdoing, or better, over some inherent wrongness in myself, I must believe I deserve to be pun-ished for my "sins," a punishment I will dread to the same degree I believe I am guilty. Thus guilt will always be associated with fear, and must be avoided at all costs. To come close to it in ourselves is to come close to the fear of our expected punishment. It makes no difference, of course, whether the punishment is forthcoming or not. We will *believe* it is, and that belief makes it real for us.

We protect ourselves from the terrifying confrontation with this guilt through our defense mechanisms, the most important of which is projec-tion. Here, we choose to see our believed sinfulness in someone else, rather than confront it in ourselves. By projecting this guilt onto others, we now become "free" of it. Choosing to deny the source of our discom-

---

*For a fuller presentation of this issue, the reader may consult my *Forgiveness and Jesus: The Meeting Place of "A Course in Miracles" and Christianity*. Foundation for "A Course in Miracles," P.O. Box 289, Crompond, NY 10517.

fort and anxiety within, we now see its cause in another, who becomes the scapegoat onto whose guilty head we feel justified in directing our "righteous indignation." Indeed, we have all become extremely adept at this dynamic, learning how to justify our anger at those we have judged to be responsible for our own misery and unhappiness (or those with whom we identify), at whose hands we are the innocent victims. This does not deny that others frequently do things they should not, nor that in the physical and psychological world of the ego we experience pain. However, there is another way of experiencing such phenomena that does not reinforce them, but will ultimately lead us beyond them. If we honestly examine our feelings and expressions of anger, we would find to our deep chagrin that at the bottom of them all is the secret wish to blame others to avoid blaming ourselves, to get others to change so that we do not have to. While we need not always agree with what others do, our experience of anger or judgment toward them is never justified because our anger has come from this hidden desire to escape our own guilt through projection.

Of course, it does not really work that way, to our even greater chagrin. Whenever we attack another, whether in our thoughts, words, or actions, we must feel guilty, for on some level we know we have attacked the person falsely, *regardless of what was done.* This is so, even if the guilt remains out of awareness, as it does, for example, in the sociopathic personality. Thus, a vicious circle of guilt and attack is established, wherein the greater our guilt, the greater becomes our need to attack others; the more we attack, the greater our guilt. And around and around we go. It is a cycle that, once begun, cannot be stopped as long as we remain within the thought system that gave rise to it.

Despite Freud's brilliance in delineating this thought system, he did not recognize the Self that exists beyond the self that he understood better, perhaps, than anyone else. Excluding that Self excludes any hope for release from the vicious grasp of the guilt-attack cycle. Thus, to his death, Freud remained pessimistic in his personal and world views, as must any adherent of a belief system that sees no ultimate freedom from guilt, but merely accommodation to it, hoping to manage its fierce dictates as best as possible. Each of us seems forever doomed to live within this world of guilt, while at the same time believing that salvation lies in projecting this self-hatred onto others, seeing in them what we do not wish to see in ourselves.

Into this seemingly hopeless situation an Answer has come. Since we are all virtually sinking in the quicksand of our own guilt, help must come to us from outside the ego that gave rise to it. This help is the Holy Spirit, who is the extension of God into this world, leading us away from our personal hell to the Heaven that is our true home. Joining us in our distorted thinking, He teaches a different thought system. It is this new way of thinking that therapists, as models and teachers, can represent to their patients as they represent it to themselves. Forgiveness is its key principle.

Forgiveness systematically reverses the ego's thought system until its fundamental premise, the reality of guilt, is undone. Basically, forgiveness does nothing except *un*do. The repressed guilt, when projected onto someone else, is now available to be reexamined and corrected. Thus, were it not for the opportunity offered by a person or situation which brings out the ''worst'' in us—our feared guilt—we would never know the self-hatred that lurks within us. Thus, our perceived enemies are those we should be most grateful to: They have become the screen on which we can see reflected our own ''secret sins and hidden hates,'' as *A Course in Miracles* phrases it.

To aid us in the process of forgiveness the Holy Spirit's Voice is always present, gently reminding us that we may choose again: Where before we had chosen to see an enemy, we are free now to see a brother or sister, one with us in the family of God. The ego perceives others as unjustifiably attacking us, the innocent victims. Thus are these ''sinners'' condemned by our judgment, while unconsciously we condemn ourselves for the same ''sin.'' Although it is not always apparent in our experience, we are nonetheless familiar with the psychological truism that what makes us guilty is not what we *do* but the attack thoughts in our *mind*. Refraining from overt attack is not sufficient to undo guilt, if the underlying thought remains uncorrected. Thus, a child's repressed anger at a parent will inevitably lead to guilt if that parent suddenly is hurt, a dynamic we know as the ''omnipotence of thought.''

The Holy Spirit corrects the ego's perception, for His judgment sees in the apparent attack a call for help. The Bible teaches that perfect love casts out fear. If one is filled with love one cannot be afraid, for love and fear are mutually exclusive states, as are love and attack, light and darkness. Thus, if one is afraid or seeks to harm another, we may conclude that that person had chosen to be separate from love, for no one who is aware of God's love could ever attack. If someone is attacking, regardless of the mode of expression, the Holy Spirit teaches us to hear this underlying statement: ''I feel alienated from God, who cannot possibly love such a miserable sinner. The only way to escape my guilt and terror is by attacking you, projecting my own perceived sinfulness. Please show me through your response that I am wrong; that I am forgiven and that God loves me.'' Thus, attack is understood as an expression of fear, and fear is a call for the love that has been denied.

In summary, forgiveness is the vision of the Holy Spirit, which He asks us to share. If we choose to judge against another, we are choosing to judge against ourselves, strengthening the prison of guilt in which we both live. However, in choosing to hear the Holy Spirit's judgment—reinterpreting what we have judged against—we are choosing to hear the Voice of forgiveness tell *us* that our sins have been forgiven.

II

The application of these principles for psychotherapy can be divided in-to three sections. In the first, we shall consider how therapists view their patients' presenting problems. Secondly, we discuss the therapists' view of themselves in the therapy. Finally we consider the role of the Holy Spirit in psychotherapy.

1. The presenting problem that brings people to therapy, regardless of its many forms, is feeling victimized by others, the world, even God. In-deed, one can say that this is the problem of each of us who walks this earth. Who are there who can say that they have never felt unfairly treated, and that the cause of their unhappiness rests with others or with forces beyond their control? We all hope somehow to remedy the pain of our lives by focusing on what seem to be external problems, rather than by making the internal changes that inevitably are more painful.

On one level, therefore, the verbal content of therapy consists of help-ing patients understand that they are not victims of the world in which they live. For example, people holding grievances against their parents can understand that while there is nothing they can do to change what hap-pened when they were children, they *can* change how they are reacting to the past *now.* This does not necessarily mean that their parents were "justified" in mistreating them, if such has been the case, but it does mean that the children, now fully grown, can look at their parents differently and forgive them. Difficult situations in childhood—or in adulthood for that matter—become opportunities for learning that we would be happier by letting go of the hurts of the past, rather than by righteously defending our grievances.

Therapists are hardly immune from seeing themselves as victims. As we all have experienced, most patients invariably "act out" against their therapist. Because the therapist is seen as threatening the patient's most prized possession—the cherished belief system that created the prob-lems—the therapist is perceived as a threat too. In return for what is ex-perienced as an attack—a perception not always in awareness—the patient will attack in return. We are all more than familiar with these defensive maneuvers: coming late for appointments, subtle verbal "digs," failure to make payments, and so forth. How therapists react to these "attacks" is critical for therapeutic progress, for themselves as well as for their pa-tients.

If the therapist reacts defensively, whether verbally, behaviorally, or on the level of thought, patients' guilt for their "attacks" is reinforced. The patient's belief in the guilt-attack cycle, evidenced by the victim-victimizer dichotomy, is demonstrated. Each has taught the other that guilt and attack are both real and justified, and thus therapist and patient remain trapped in guilt, and true healing becomes impossible.

If, however, therapists do not perceive the patient's "acting out" as an attack—in other words, do not take it personally—then their nondefensive reaction teaches the patient that there has been no attack, only a call for help. The best teaching is by example, and here therapists are given the opportunity to act as models for their verbal teaching. Throughout history the greatest spiritual teachers have been those who lived what they taught, not merely uttered spiritual truths. The guilty King Claudius exclaims in *Hamlet*, "Words without thoughts never to heaven go." The popular phrase, "Do as I say, not as I do," has never inspired the true spiritual aspirant.

Thus do we see therapy's most demanding challenge: meeting attack without defense. How we as therapists meet this challenge determines not only what we teach our patients, but what we teach ourselves. The purpose of therapy is to help therapist *and* patient learn that they are not victims of each other, but only of themselves.

2. One of our major mistakes in living in this world is to confuse role with content. Although we do live in a world of roles, our task is to be *in* them, yet remembering that we are not *of* them. Roles separate and keep us separate, obscuring the underlying unity that is our natural inheritance as children of one Creator, joined in the love that transcends all forms. As therapists, we run the risk of believing in the role of therapist, that it is the people coming to us who need healing, not ourselves. The therapist-patient format can reinforce this, obscuring our mutual need for each other.

Countertransference has usually been regarded as a negative phenomenon, especially in more traditional therapy where the therapist is taught to be objective, detached, and emotionally uninvolved with the patient; to be, in other words, a blank screen onto which patients will project (transfer) their unconscious needs and demands. At the same time it is incumbent on the therapist to do just the opposite. In reality, however, this is impossible. Whatever is in our mind must be projected, whether it is our love or our guilt. Thus we all project, and all the time. In this sense, transference and countertransference are one and the same. While we are not free of this law, we *are* free to choose what we will project: guilt or forgiveness, sickness or healing.

Rather than seeing their reactions to the patient—annoyance, fear, guilt, concern, sexuality, discomfort, and so forth—as negative, as the term countertransference is usually understood, therapists would recognize that their patient was sent to them so that these very reactions would occur, bringing to the surface what had been repressed. When therapists' "buttons are pushed," the patient is no longer seen as the *cause* of these reactions, but rather as the means of bringing them to the surface. Thus, therapists too are patients. Both people have been brought together to accept the opportunity offered by the Holy Spirit to join together and be healed by Him, seeing in each other the mirror of the self they would rather deny and avoid.

4

8

The paradox here is obvious. On the one hand, therapists are asked to recognize their own need for healing. On the other hand, this mutual healing occurs within the context of the *form* of therapy wherein they offer help to the patient. This paradox is observed in all forms of help or service, be they education, law, medicine, religious ministry, parenting, and so forth. All are differing forms of expressing the principle we have already considered: to be *in* the role but not *of* it. We act as the role dictates, yet never losing sight of the purpose of forgiveness that is being served.

3. Examining our Judeo-Christian roots, we see that the beginning of the cosmic drama which culminates in salvation is the act of disobedience against God known as "Original Sin." Central to "sin" is the belief that we have not only separated ourselves from God, but have usurped His role as Creator, as we observed in the beginning of this article. Thus, we have come to believe that we are God, which mistake is the true meaning of the "authority problem." Psychotherapy affords therapists the unique and powerful opportunity to correct this misperception by avoiding the temptation to believe that they are the therapists or healers. We have seen that as therapists we share the same need for forgiveness as do our patients. And indeed, it is the practice of therapy that gives us the chance to *be* forgiven. To believe that we know what is best for someone else, or to believe that we possess special knowledge, ability, or power is the same problem—"Who is the Author of our reality?"—that underlies all our problems, personally and collectively. Recognizing that we are not the therapist is the invitation to the Holy Spirit that He be the therapist.

* * *

Borrowing Shakespeare's metaphor that all the world is a stage, we understand that we have taken the role of therapist in order to learn Who the real Therapist is. As therapists, we are afforded a rare opportunity, even a privilege, to focus on the very source of our problems: the distorted thinking about ourselves and our Creator. Joining with one who shares the inherent loneliness of a life of separation, suffering, and death, we undo our own belief in separate interests and are healed together, fulfilling the Holy Spirit's purpose. Accepting His gift we accept the happy news that we are not alone; God's love and peace are restored to our awareness, and in His love we are healed together. This unity through forgiveness is the condition of knowing the peace of God, which is the ultimate goal of all psychotherapy.

REFERENCE

A Course in miracles. (1975). Tiburon, CA: Foundation for Inner Peace (P.O. Box 635).

Change in the Client
and in the Client's God

Albert S. Rossi

A colleague of mine is fond of saying, "In psychotherapy, when God changes, we change." The process of therapy usually accomplishes multilevel goals simultaneously. Clients with deeply religious convictions often experience what they call "progress toward God" as therapy unfolds. One of the ways clients understand this is through their image of God.

Andrea, a deeply committed religious person, found that during the early stages of therapy she became simultaneously confused and reluctantly accepting of her confusion. She used religious categories to describe this as "the dark journey into the soul." Classical psychoanalysis refers to this as "the process of making the unconscious conscious." The darkness lifted after a lengthy period of therapy. Andrea then said, "I finally began to understand the implications of my alcoholic father's behavior. And I also know that I sometimes don't trust God. In a crisis I have a gut feeling that God is going to let me down. That's just like my father. And that's something to work with."

The beginning of the venture into the land of the unconscious is often unsettling. The client often expresses this as an uncertainty about therapy. The religiously committed client often has doubts about therapy anyway and will probably be helped by some reinforcement for being willing to come this far. For the religiously committed client, the axiom, "Beginning therapy is more than half the battle," often means having made the decision to reflect upon all aspects of one's life, including religious ones. As therapy goes along, the issue often focuses upon the difference between early religious education and later life experiences. The symbol for this growth often is the client's image of God.

Adult clients often cling to childhood images of God. As the client becomes more familiar and adept at walking into the land of the unconscious, he or she often becomes more willing to examine that childhood image of God. The client then often expresses the awareness of the true

Albert S. Rossi received his PhD in school psychology from Hofstra University in 1976. He is a practicing clinical psychologist in White Plains, New York, and teaches at Pace University in Pleasantville, New York.

55

unknowability of God, of His transcendence. In the latter stages of therapy the client is able to articulate the growth of knowing that God is more distant and more present at the same time. God is sometimes referred to as the Infinite Sustainer. By and large, I have found clients express a conviction, even when they know that they don't know much about God, that they have a more personal relationship with Him in the latter stages of therapy.

One of my thumbnail operating definitions in therapy is, "Maturity is the ability to live with ambiguity." For the religiously committed client, this becomes quite threatening because it means losing control of treasured areas of life, including the control of God's power over the life of the client.

The client then becomes more willing to continue therapy, to enter the doorway of the unconscious, come what may. The client has less need to control therapy, less need to control life generally. Then the client has less need for an authoritarian hold on her or his image of God. The client begins to be willing to live with more doubt and uncertainty. In *The Brothers Karamazov,* Dostoyevsky (1950) has the youngest brother, saintly Alexey, speak as the conscience of the family. Alexey, as he advances in the monastic life, finally says, "And perhaps I don't even believe in God" (p. 229). Alexey could articulate this real doubt and he could articulate deep faith in his Church and in God. This willingness to be honest about one's real faith in a real God opens the way for new insights into the real nature of faith as lived.

Mary Ellen, a particularly succinct client, put it rather well. She said, "You see, I have a problem of control. I like to see problems solved and ambiguities clarified. I don't like to leave things to chance. The result is, I sometimes forget who is really in charge. In other words, I don't always trust God."

Mary Ellen put into words the struggle of most of my religiously oriented clients. I am reminded of a comment made by a prominent theologian (whose name I cannot remember), "When some of us die we are going to be surprised we aren't God." Religiously committed clients often come closer to their own humanity as they include a reexamination of their sense of God. This insight is often a powerful and hope-giving discovery for the client.

THE CASE OF LISA

A highly committed religious woman, Lisa, told me at the beginning of her psychotherapy, "I've always tried to make my life tidy and it isn't working." The connotation of "tidy" was unmistaken. She wanted her life to be regular, neat, and upright, with all the positive attributes she associated with that. In her present prayer life she had the feeling of suspended animation. She said she thought she would pray better when she had her life more in order. Her prayer life, like the rest of her life, was being lived in the future. Lisa hadn't been able to reflect clearly on the negative side of her idea of tidy and to face her irrational need for control and her perfectionistic tendencies. When she came for therapy Lisa said she was "confused and unhappy."

Lisa's therapy included the unraveling of her psychological makeup and her religious belief system. Lisa was a single woman in her mid-40s. Her mother was a caring woman, given to excessive demands and sometimes punishing by using excessively guilt-laden statements. Lisa's father was a passive, enigmatic figure in her childhood who died when she was 13. After his death, Lisa's mother told her that he was a "difficult man to live with." She said he occasionally acted out his transvestite fantasy when the two of them were alone. Lisa found this news to be disconcerting. She became angry with her dead father and had a confusing reaction to her mother. Lisa repressed all this and attempted to continue to live her life as usual. When Lisa came for therapy she said she was beginning to understand that she had an unconscious doubt about her femininity since her early adolescence, and probably earlier.

Like many of my other clients, Lisa found sustenance in being able to discuss her concerns in psychological rather than moral terms. Her moral background was Roman Catholic and quite legalistic. Another client, Tom, with somewhat the same religious background, came for short-term therapy. Tom was a high-level university administrator who came for therapy because he was "uneasy." After a few sessions Tom expressed great delight in using psychological categories rather than moral categories. His new translation was that he was not "scrupulous" but had "perfectionistic tendencies." He said he now understood himself not as "morally rigid" but as "compulsive." This reformulation released immense energy for Tom. His self-concept was based upon well-worn religious clichés which had nothing left to offer him. As he attempted to assess his current state of mind, he became circular and depressed. I have found this to be true of many religiously oriented clients. Psychological categories provide the perspective within which they can conceive of themselves taking new risks. Tom and Lisa returned to moral categories, but with a new attitude toward themselves and their image of God.

Lisa required a rather lengthy period of therapy to uncover and deal with her feelings toward her father, and then toward her mother. This period involved a predictable span of labile mood swings. She became elated with her new courage to face the past and the insights she found. Alternately, she became depressed with the implications of these insights for her current struggle. Her relationships with her few friends became uncertain. Her night dreams and her daydreams began to change.

On the cognitive level Lisa's therapy involved a gradual unraveling of her self-statements in the present. She slowly began to realize that her past had left her with an ongoing inner dialogue of perfectionistic directives. She began to organize her new search around psychological concepts. She began to find herself saying to herself statements like, "I should laugh more than I do" and "I should come closer to perfection as I get older." These cognitions were, of course, depressive and depressing.

Her mounting depression had caused her a new problem. Lately she had taken to spending time in her room alone, nude. She began to spend lengthy periods of time in front of the mirror viewing herself. She referred to this as her "compulsion" and became quite depressed when she "gave in to it" and was quite unable to stop doing it. For Lisa, this was overwhelming. She had always been able to live her life within a rather restricted moral code. Now she was not even able to do that.

On a behavioral level, Lisa's therapy included new risks with her few friends. She had always strategized her relationships so that she remained subordinate, at times infantile. She needed those close to her to be dominant. Lisa had a terror of growing up psychologically because she wasn't sure that, underneath it all, she was a woman. She knew how to remain a girl but she had serious inhibitions about becoming a responsible, adult woman.

She slowly took the risk of expressing an unwelcome opinion to her closest friend. Then she began to make legitimate requests of her new friends. For her, these changes were momentous. As it turned out, Lisa lost the friendship of her closest friend. Lisa also realized that this breakup was healthy and long overdue.

Simultaneously, she was making significant attitudinal changes. Lisa began to reflect upon her image of her father and her mother. She described this reflection as "finally facing who they were, and forgiving them." Her anger toward her father was greater than she imagined. Her resentment toward her mother had taken the form of mild sarcasm toward women authority figures. Lisa finally saw the connection between her doubts about her femininity and the way her father treated her.

Toward the end of her therapy Lisa said, "I don't have a clear image of God anymore. I know my life is difficult and, realistically, it doesn't look like it will get any easier." Her 81-year-old aunt, who lived with Lisa's mother, became increasingly sickly and demanding. Although Lisa didn't live with the two older women, she was their primary caretaker. Lisa added, "I do know that I'm not worried because God will provide." Her assertion was very direct and very clear. It was also very different from her assertion about God when she began therapy.

She found that to be very freeing. She said she was now ready to be more open to the God of Revelation and less dependent upon her fixed projections. She became more able to live with an ambiguous and unclear, but real, awareness of God as opposed to her need to control God by fixating his image on the primary authority figure in her life, her father.

Although uneven, Lisa's therapy involved living with more ambiguity about her own private life, not knowing if and when her compulsion would disappear.

She was able to say that at first, she "felt rotten" about herself when she gave in to her compulsion. Later she was able to make the connection between her behavior and her childhood doubts. She began to accept herself more within the real circumstances of her life.

Lisa's therapy also included a reevaluation of her religious belief system. She said she didn't "switch religions," she did "switch her mind to a new understanding of Catholicism." She began to untangle her image of God and her memory of her father.

One of the highlights for Lisa was the change in her expectation of a tidy life. She began to scrutinize her life under the magnifying glass of perfectionistic tendencies. This helped her organize her search. She quickly understood that she interpreted the Bible quote, "Be ye perfect as your Heavenly Father is perfect," in a strict, literal sense. She had applied the American cultural connotation of the word "perfect" to the Bible quote. Thus, she was trying to be perfect "through flawless accomplishments and unerring performances." She also began to realize that the word perfect in American culture refers to an evaluation of the past, not an assessment of an event in progress. A ballet is perfect only when it is over. A baseball game is pitched perfectly only after the last batter is out. The word perfect refers to something final which cannot change.

Another spiritual guideline which Lisa revisited was from a 12th-century book called *The Imitation of Christ* (Kempis, 1955). An important admonition in Lisa's life had been the quote, "If a man were to get rid of one fault a year, he would soon be a perfect man" (p. 43). When she was young, this was music to her ears. It was filled with hope and promise. Now that she was in midlife she could view the admonition in a new light. The results of this reexamination were confusing.

I have found that many religiously inclined clients have blended their personal anxiety with selected religious teachings to produce a unique, rarified form of perfectionistic obsessions and compulsive behaviors. The breakdown of this system often occurs in midlife, when the system can be viewed in light of many years' experience. In Lisa's attempt to become perfect according to *The Imitation of Christ,* she concluded that, now, in her mid-40s she was "behind schedule," to use her words.

Lisa went back to the Bible to examine the quote, "Be ye perfect as your Heavenly Father is perfect." This time she began to understand and underline the word "as." She understood that "as" doesn't relate to the American cultural notion of flawless behavior or accomplishments without error. For Lisa, the word "as" related to the life of God the Father as revealed. After some reflection and discussion she summarized her new conclusion about the life of the Father with the word "compassionate." She now saw herself as being perfect as the Father is perfect (compassionate). For her, this shifted her evaluation. She understood that she was called to be compassionate, not behaviorally flawless, and that her compassion extended to herself. This also put her concept of sinfulness in a new perspective.

Much later Lisa said she understood that she was as sinful now as she was 20 years ago. She also understood that this wasn't a problem. She said it might even be progress. She now said she could understand that she is malicious, envious, narcissistic, and much more. Her conclusion was that her consciousness had expanded, not that she had grown worse.

Lisa, single and having no prospect for marriage, said she now understood how she was very severely limited when it came to loving. She began to understand that love and sexuality are, by their very nature, a result of a developmental process. Viktor Frankl (1978) referred to this as "progressive maturation" (p. 81). Lisa began to understand her own serious developmental lag. She said she even understood that 20 years ago she hoped to do everything for the love of God. Now she wondered if she did anything purely for the love of God. She smiled when she said it, noting that she had a peace about it all. She said much of the Bible was taking on a new perspective. She said that she was beginning to come to the "truth" and that after much pain, the truth was really freeing for her.

Lisa's image of God underwent a slow transformation. She knew clearly what her image of God had been. She also knew that she didn't know what this image would become. She stated quite clearly, "In my drive to make my life tidy I was playing God."

Late in Lisa's therapy she took delight in quoting back to me from an article of mine I had given her at the beginning of therapy. Her quote was her summary of her new view of herself.

> Real people seem infinitely complex, infinitely inadequate, infinitely redeemed, which opens the possibility of being infinitely loved and loving. . . . We are all inferior in major ways. We are all fallen, part of the walking wounded. We are all terminally ill. Today. And the joy is that Christ came to salvage us from the plight. (Rossi, 1982, p. 250)

Lisa added, "That's me, except for the part about being infinitely loved and loving. I don't know if I'll ever understand that." But Lisa was now willing to live with the ambiguity of not knowing if she would ever understand it.

The case of Lisa is the presentation of the psychological struggle and real growth stages of many of my clients. Some of the case has been altered for the sake of greater comprehension. The fundamental thrust of Lisa's growth has been paralleled by many other religiously committed persons.

CONCLUSION

Religiously oriented clients usually respond well to metaphor, paradox, parable, and image. I have found great use for some of the parables and stories handed down in the various religious traditions. For cases like Lisa, one of the better stories comes from Yalom (1975).

> In this Hassidic story a rabbi is having a conversation with God about heaven and hell. The rabbi asks what hell is like. The Lord responds with, "I will show you hell." He leads the rabbi into a room with a large round table in the center. Around the table sit starving people who are desperate, complaining, and bitter. In the center of the table was a steaming pot of delicious stew. The rabbi's mouth began to water. Each person had a long spoon which could reach into the pot to dip into the stew. However, the spoon was longer than the human arm so the person couldn't put the stew into his/her mouth. The persons in the group are starving. Then the Lord says, "Now I will show you heaven." He leads the rabbi into the next room where a similar group of people sit, nourished, plump and healthy. The people are laughing and talking. The room has the same table, same stew, same spoons. The rabbi asked what the difference was. "It is simple but it requires a certain skill," said the Lord. "You see, they have learned to feed each other." (p. 12)

Often religiously oriented clients haven't really grasped the equality of persons suggested by this story. For many, the reality of giving and taking of food—emotional sustenance—is a major problem. The religiously oriented client, particularly one with perfectionistic tendencies, often feels most comfortable in a dominant-submissive relationship. This was clearly illustrated in the case of Lisa. The client can be comfortable living on either side of this relationship. Mutuality, as suggested in the Yalom story, often needs to be explored with religious clients. Most are quite adept at using notable quotes about mutuality, and many have posters on walls or plaques on desks proclaiming the equality of mankind. But an examination of their real intimate relationships often unearths a need to explore mutuality with the real friends they have.

The therapeutic process for religiously committed clients often includes an examination of their perfectionistic tendencies. These are sometimes uncovered through the process of dealing with compulsive behaviors and legalistic expectations. One of the consequences, psychologically, for the client is an experiential growth in mutuality in close friendships. Oftentimes, a barometer of the psychological change is the client's image of God. "In psychotherapy, when God changes, we change" becomes quite real to clients as they embrace their humanity more.

REFERENCES

Dostoyevsky, F. (1950). *The brothers Karamazov.* New York: The Modern Library.

Frankl, V. (1978). *The unheard cry for meaning.* New York: Simon and Schuster.

Kempis, T. (1955). *The imitation of Christ.* Garden City, NY: Image Books.

Rossi, A. (1982). Learning from our mistakes. *Studies in Formative Spirituality,* 3(2), 245-252.

Yalom, I. (1975). *The theory and practice of group psychotherapy,* (2nd ed.). New York: Basic Books.

Latent Theology:
A Clinical Perspective on
The Future of an Illusion

Gary Ahlskog

No one who had a childhood has a liberal theology. Freud (1927/1964) grasped this point so simply in *The Future of an Illusion* that his sophisticated understanding of religion in psychic structure has received insufficient appreciation. This paper amplifies but does not improve upon Freud. He clearly saw how modern theologies with their admixtures of philosophical and existential underpinnings would generate endless elaborations upon abstract religious ideas. He just as clearly dismissed them as an "intellectual misdemeanor" that can "stretch the meaning of words until they retain scarcely anything of their original sense" (p. 51), resulting in theologies that are either "nothing more than an insubstantial shadow and no longer the mighty personality of religious doctrines" (p. 52), or that persist in calling religious any humble acquiescence in "the small part which human beings play in the world" (p. 52). That, of course, Freud called "irreligious in the truest sense of the word" (p. 52).

Although there is much that could be explored in Freud's discussion of the secondary functions of religion—exorcizing by humanizing the forces of nature, reconciling people to the cruelty of fate and death, compensating them for the privations of civilized life (p. 24)—this paper focuses on Freud's understanding of the role of religion within individual psychic structure. His position is easily summarized, less easily explicated. Thanks to childhood education, usually a program devoted to "retardation of sexual development and premature religious influence" (p. 78), the precepts of civilized life, which are originally experienced as coercions, become internalized by "a special mental agency, man's superego," which agency appropriately transforms the child from an "opponent" of civilization into one of its "vehicles" (p. 13). Freud always intended superego as an aspect of ego, a distinct ego capacity for acculturation, the capacity to digest the ideals, permissions, and restraints

Gary Ahlskog, PhD, is a licensed psychologist and psychoanalyst practicing in New York City, and the director of the Pastoral Counseling Training Program at Postgraduate Center for Mental Health. He is a faculty member and supervisor in this and other psychoanalytic training programs.

that communal life prescribes in the service of preserving communal pleasure and safety. However, the potential alliance between ego and superego, which is clinically recognizable to the extent that individuals adopt a friendly attitude to rules and restraints that generally serve their own interests (p. 68), is confounded by the child's, or the patient's, naive or neurotic assimilation of meaning systems. Freud objected to religious indoctrination, of course, but he noted *en passant* similar objections to American Manifest Destiny (pp. 27, 80-81), Marxism (p. 76), and the Monarchy (p. 79) on the grounds that meaning systems, that is, the investing of otherwise negotiable guidelines with "a quite special solemnity" (p. 66), represent an infantile or desperate method of mobilizing the superego to tame passions through force—the force of repression or, one might say, suppression. Thus, religion cannot help but represent the "universal obsessional neurosis of humanity" (p. 71), since theological systems promote unverifiable claims of ideal purpose, meaning, and value as a replacement for the individual's negotiated pleasures in everyday affairs.

These remarks become clearer when cast in their more radical form. The potential alliance between ego and superego is so disrupted by theology that the ego's regulation of *gratification* is opposed by the superego's vague but powerful claims of *meaning*. Gratification here means the aligning of aim and object to discharge tension with minimal anxiety, minimal threat of symptom or unpleasure, and thus it is synonymous with the dually maximized achievements of pleasure and safety. Meaning is here restricted in definition to any alteration of behavior, thought, or feeling brought about by the individual's accommodation of force, or the threat of force, whether real or imagined. So, for example, the displeasure of a parent has, in the life of a small child, a significantly greater meaning (altering force) than the displeasure of a colleague typically has in the life of an adult. The colleague's displeasure is likely to be more interesting, reflecting, say, disagreements over politics, economics, ethics, taste, or nuances of daily life; but such interests belong to the colloquial or philosophical definitions of meaning and are of no concern here. The child's accommodation to parental power occurs despite the fact that issues such as where to play or how much noise to make are of little philosophical interest.

The true counterpoint of meaning is not nihilism but flexibility. No one who had a childhood has a liberal theology because theology, to the extent that it proposes obligatory solemnity to any of life's forms, supercedes at best—and at worst, opposes—personally negotiated gratifications. Freud's "education to reality" (pp. 81 ff.) proposed an experiment in which personal gratification, pursuit, and restraint thereof, could become the subject of life in its own right. He was obviously familiar with some of the developments of liberal theology in the late 19th and early 20th centuries, but he found himself unable to conclude that any such developments were actually used in the service of expanded gratifications. If, in the absence of the force of indoctrination, people were found to generate religious faiths, either because they needed them for safety or wanted them for pleasure, then Freud was quite prepared to abandon his stance (p. 80). The whole experiment remains destined to fail, however, as long as meaning systems, whether theological, astrological, political, whether systematically verfiable or not, can oppose it with the force of foregone, presanctified conclusions. During childhood education superego plays a subliminal joke on ego. Prudence, flexibility, and negotiability are only illusions offered to the developing individual. Actually, the power of the superego's meaning systems will inexorably prevail. ''I talk openly about everything with Jennifer, I want her to feel good about herself sexually. In 10 years when she's 16, that's what scares me.''

Latent theology as used here is a double entendre that refers first to the reappearance, during psychotherapeutic treatment, of childhood religious ideas, ideals, and memories seemingly discarded in adult life. The content of such religious issues is usually quite accessible to patients and can become an occasion for them to blame elders for harsh, rigid, or whimsical attitudes inflicted during formative years. Also, childhood religion may be cited as a major source of guilt or self-doubt concerning impulses to aggression, competition, success, masturbation, seductiveness, conquest, coital pleasure, leisure, and the like.

> The patient, a moderately successful architect, mocked and attacked his sadistic Irish father and parochial-school teachers for branding as sinful his intellectual achievements, enjoyed at the expense of others with less ability. He also mocked and attacked himself during treatment hours for bypassing commissions because of fits of anxiety or symptomatic acts that prevented enjoyment of ''more than (his) share.'' In his manifest irreligion this residue of a seemingly discarded religious upbringing became a vehicle for expressing oedipal defeat, as he demonstrated repeatedly to himself that his manifest irreligion must defer to their stronger religion. He consciously disavowed this religion but unconsciously convicted himself according to its precepts, thus framing an obsessive defense against personal pleasure that spiraled downward into ever more subtle, more complicated inner defeats.

This first definition of latent theology as the reemergence of childhood religious themes to express oedipal (or preoedipal) conflicts is reasonably uncomplicated and simply attests to the fact that religious content from one's personal childhood remains a vehicle through which psychic conflicts are repeated and eventually remembered. Of course, political themes could serve as a vehicle too, as illustrated by a similar treatment struggle on the part of a man whose parents were members of an underground leftist movement. His productive university career as a botanist was confounded by lapses of attention to routine financial affairs so that he was repeatedly faced with evictions and minor court appearances. Inordinate complications in these types of treatment arise mainly when therapists collude with manifest assertions to the effect that their patients have already neutralized the manifest foibles of their parents. Besides being inaccurate from a structural viewpoint, such collusion robs patients of the most accessible vehicle for talking about themselves.

The second definition of latent theology pertains less to the content of childhood religious themes than to a persistent quest for and/or belief in the eventual validity of *some* theology. This is the more complicated problem of religion within individual psychic structure that Freud grasped so clearly. Space carved out in the psyche during childhood for presanctified meaning systems must be analyzed or it will inexorably be filled. If not filled in later years with manifestly religious doctrines, then it will be filled more idiosyncratically with admixtures of personal and/or social ideas and/or ideals. Whatever its content, the function of these new guidelines is to retain the parameters of a force field developed during childhood.

> A patient 11 years outside the convent produced little religious material over the hours. As far as she was concerned, past religious teachings were a bit silly but over and done with. Instead, she was embarked upon a quest to experience "wholeness," pursued with intense guilt and self-criticism. Contemporary psychologies contained for her essential revelations about the nature of "really being a person." Yet these revelations were seemingly unrealizable for her through an ordinary (imperfect) sexual relationship and productive work life. The space originally carved out for religious doctrines was refilled with the solemn principles of "assertiveness" and "self-actualization" that, clinically speaking, forced her actions in the same way that religious indoctrination once did. In the transference she found herself "unredeemed" but "devoted to" complying with the dictates of modern psychology. Existential philosophies regarding the condition of human alienation poorly rationalized the clinically observable power of her superego, newly armed with psychology, diverting her away from the gratifications available to her in the name of the higher meaning of being mentally healthy.

In this version of a religious obsession, a psychological meaning system warded off the patient's impending sense of danger at the prospect that maximum pleasure and safety could themselves be the subject of her life.

It is no easy task for a therapist to crystallize the latent theological system of a patient. Logic and grammar are not isomorphic to psychic structure. As in the case above, what sounds like the grammar of ego liberation can serve the function of reintroducing a superego force field in more disguised form. A useful oversimplification in this regard is that the superego can conscript any available grammar of ideal meanings in the service of restricting affect, where affect is understood in its broadest sense to refer to the complete spectrum of tension discharges that comprise pleasurable experience and self-expression. Latent theology narrows this spectrum, that is, restricts ego options for organizing id, and substitutes instead compliance to approved meanings that may frequently be misconstrued as "insight." For example, the misfortune of an enemy permits a delicious moment for expanded pleasurable discharge, as in the case of a patient who found herself gleefully and unexpectedly singing, "I don't care, I don't care, I don't care." The architect mentioned earlier, however, responded to a similar situation saying, "There's something here, odd. I don't feel particularly bad; it's like the realization that maybe I wanted it. And I don't feel guilty like I thought. I'm maybe getting in touch with a sadistic side of me, but I haven't worked that out yet." This response is in no way insight, but rather a repetitive constriction of gratification in deference to newly conceived meanings. His latent concept of temporal sanctification here retains its structural role of transforming pleasure into meaning by force. Crystallizing these kinds of systems requires the therapist to hear the difference between a patient's expanding personal language of gratification and repetitive compliance with any sanctified meaning systems.

With scholarship and piercing imagination, Roustang (1980) has concluded that psychoanalytic theory itself belongs in the category of a debilitating meaning system. The therapist's theory is just as deadly as religious dogma, for as the theory swells to the status of a truth—an inexorable law instead of a poignant fiction—it lures desperate patients toward compliance, dependency, and then toward doomed attempts at rebellion that can only lead to interminable estrangement, and interminable treatment. This paradox, that the patient desires to find in the therapist a knowing other whose very existence then invalidates the self, is only soluble if the therapist is boldly willing to venture what Roustang calls distance errors, that is, flawed approaches to the patient's subjectivity which are neither so caring as to become enveloping nor so competent that they reinfantalize the patient through their sheer impassability. Such a flawed and therefore therapeutic encounter does not permit the therapist to betray the patient by retreat to the higher ground of reified psychoanalytic knowledge. In this essential abandonment of prearranged knowledge, prearranged values, a prearranged professional identity, and even the Freudian pericope, the therapist, along with the patient, risks nothing less than psychosis itself.

Only where there is no meaning, that is, where nothing makes prearranged sense, does the possibility arise for that intensely personal, separate, non-contingent, autonomous voice—the patient's "I"—that heals through its very alterneity.

So the patient must give up theology and the therapist must give up theory. The healing task is to render superfluous any need for such meaning systems at all. This is still a radical, frequently intolerable experiment, perhaps for patients and therapists alike. The need to fill the space carved out for meaning may recur in subtle allegiances to "openness," or "warmth," or "self-acceptance," or even cultivated atheism. A patient subtly drew the therapist into a reified superego meaning system by mentioning that he had impulsively committed a minor theft the week before and wanted to "get to the bottom of it." The therapist's latent wishes for meaning permitted a temporary collusion with the patient's notion that the act should be deemed a symptom, a moral misdemeanor but a psychic felony. Only when the therapist realized that the patient was using this act as evidence for long-standing fantasies of secret malevolence (and guilt) could the therapist accurately clarify the act as a derivative form of aggressive pleasure, permissible precisely because it could so easily be mislabeled a psychological symptom, that is, permissible because it was bound to be stopped by guilt, self-criticism, and pseudo-insight. In this case the therapist temporarily resisted Freud's radical experiment, in which the superego's meaning systems are totally superfluous, in which the only valid subject is the extent of gratification experienced in the events and emotions that comprise a daily life. The idea that these events and emotions need not tally into a coherent system of meaning (neither theological nor psychological) threatens an evacuation of superego that seems to foretell danger. The popular notion, even among therapists, that this fantasized danger must be respected for the sake of social order is another superego joke. Freud's point was that an unchecked ego permitted to regulate gratification is no danger at all, because hypothetically dangerous impulses from the id are assimilated by a fully functioning ego into the individual's best interests. A fully functioning ego does not need to be taught not to murder a parent and certainly does not need to be forced to refrain from it.

Patients under the grip of latent theological systems simply do not accept the prospect of this kind of personal freedom. Their defending of the superego's function is, as it were, undisguised. Having counted on the safety of meaning systems and having remained ignorant of the specific shape of their appetites for so long they envision themselves unchecked as likely savages, insatiable, unspeakably dangerous, and as without ego to serve their interests. Actually, neither Freud, therapists, nor patients can be psychic anarchists where there is ego. The possibility for structural change, rendering the superego superfluous, begins, therefore, as the patient mobilizes support for the superego's function in forcing compliance to meanings. Said a newly married patient who had abandoned for convenience her mother's long-standing instructions on the way to prepare certain meals: "I know it doesn't make any difference, but I don't want to not have the rules." Her anxiety at the prospect that convenience was, by itself, a fully adequate guide for her actions reflected a seemingly dangerous intrusion of ego into functions formerly handled by superego force. As might be predicted, analysis of this anxiety was found to encompass former restrictions on her sexual life and a convoluted prohibition against being a mother.

Mobilized support for the superego's right to force compliance is clinically observable in at least three characteristic forms. First, patients presume, without necessarily knowing that they presume, that they are surrounded by force fields, legitimate and abundant meanings, that require respect. Freud's primary forces, the cruelty of nature and the fact of death, are rarely included in the patient's list of what amount to other safer meaning fabrications. A few such fabrications include the presumptions that a broken promise causes harm, that a sexual peccadillo constitutes a character flaw, that running away makes things worse, that the majority must be respected, and that chickens come home to roost. None of these minor meaning fabrications can be shown to have durable validity, nor are they trustable guides amid particular human events. Nevertheless they can be mistaken for basic truths to which the patient expects to submit, ironically in the name of clearheadedness. Second, patients frequently disavow abundant evidence in their lives testifying to their essentially nondangerous desires and essentially nondangerous means of regulating them. Third, they protest that without some form of trustable meaning, life could be only unceasing chaos or despair. These latter two mobilizations may usefully be clarified as instances of infantile grandiosity. Certainly it is as hard to play Satan as it is to play God. Clarification, however, only sets the stage for the necessary, complete interpretation of the latent theological system itself.

Latent theology as here discussed reflects the structural clash between two opposing psychic functions: the pursuit of gratification and the preservation of the threat of force, each competing to define and stabilize daily life. Through the oedipal paradigm Freud demonstrated repeatedly that the threat of force is cherished and defended to the extent that its loss would threaten an invitation to formerly repressed desires in the proscribed realms of murder and incest. The uniquely valid enforcement of these prohibitions occurred in childhood through the parents' stronger counter-wishes and unavailability. Except for this unique force and enforcement, the regulation of the individual's sexual and aggressive drives no longer requires force and may safely come under the supervision of ego in the individual's best interests. This regulation or supervision promotes, most notably, the capacity for choice in the pursuit or restraint of impulses.

Interpretation of latent theological conflict centers, therefore, on the archaic wish to rely on force (of meanings) rather than the self's own choice to pursue or proscribe in the self's own interest. Oedipal conflict can be analyzed but never analyzed away, since this conflict recurs throughout life. Interpretation aims to place recurring conflict permanently within the arena of self-interested choice and no longer within the arena of compliance to any system of meanings, powers, ideals, or even values. In other words, the instincts remain essentially unknowable. They may seem to be naively mastered by moral force, or they may during development or through analysis be permitted derivative forms regulated by the ego in the best interests of the individual's pleasure and safety. Where, one might ask, is the danger, chaos, or despair in that?

Freud's experiment may not soon reshape childhood education, but it is to be considered a nondangerous experiment in the treatment room. Ironically, this experiment that insists upon obviating the function of childhood theologies permits unfettered experiences of religious faith when pursued for gratification. To acknowledge this is not to sanction at the end of this paper another subtle meaning system. Fundamental issues regarding self, other, and the world—its promises and its illusions—are contained within the theology of the ages; yet Holmer (1984) has correctly noted that one must have cultivated a self capable of passionately addressing this material before it can make any sense. Theology will not and cannot create the capacity. Kierkegaard's (1843/1946) Knight of Faith, who has cultivated the capacity for pleasure in an afternoon walk and has outgrown the need to grasp the infinite mysteries of life, might qualify for a psychoanalytic saint, if only he were a living being and not one of Kierkegaard's brilliant fictions. Freud's point, happily, is that the eradication of the threat of meaning makes sainthood universal—and blessedly ordinary.

REFERENCES

Freud, S. (1964). *The future of an illusion* (W.D. Robson Scott, Trans., J. Strachey, Ed.). Garden City: Doubleday. (Original work published in 1927.)

Holmer, P. (1984). *Making Christian sense.* Philadelphia: The Westminster Press.

Kierkegaard, S. (1946). Fear and trembling. In R. Bretall (Ed.), *A Kierkegaard anthology* (pp. 116-134). New York: Modern Library. (Original work published in 1843.)

Roustang, F. (1980). *Psychoanalysis never lets go* (N. Lukacher, Tr.). Baltimore, MD: The Johns Hopkins University Press.

The Play of Illusion as an Opening to the Future of the Self: Reflections of a Religious Clinician Occasioned by Rereading *The Future of an Illusion*

Vivienne Joyce

The experience of time is a dimension of subjectivity, and time and timing are intrinsic elements in the art and science of psychotherapy. The complex interrelationships of id, ego, and superego are matched by the complex interrelationships of past, present, and future that are common to both psychoanalysis and religious experience as recorded in Western Scriptures. Certainly it is taken for granted that the past lives in the present and that individual development requires a coming to know and to feel the past giving shape to the present/future self. Forgetting and recalling are part of the formative and creative processes of therapeutic work and of the Biblical account of salvation history.

In *Civilization and Its Discontents,* Freud stated that perhaps he did not concern himself enough with one of the sources of religious experience—what his friend Romain Rolland called a sensation of "eternity." Along with a loss of ego boundaries, these feelings involved a sense of an intimate loving bond between the ego and the world. In "Comments on Religious Experience," Loewald (1978, p.64) describes moments of exceptional intensity—orgasm, bliss, despair, when there seems only to be a "now"—as experiences that are of time but not in time: moments complete in themselves. All there is is in the experience: the eternal now of which theologians speak. This is another realm of experiencing that is not just defensive but can be used defensively. In a religious context "eternity" points to divine mystery—Otherness. Ecclesiastes laments the nature of time without eternity. The believing Jew and Christian assert that the Eternal God is revealed in time. Loewald suggests that time without eter-

Vivienne Joyce, SC, CSW, is a certified social worker and psychoanalytic psychotherapist in private practice in New York City and the Assistant Director of the Pastoral Counseling Training Program at the Postgraduate Center for Mental Health.

71

nity is like consciousness (secondary process) torn from its connectedness
to the unconscious (primary process). Today it is difficult to think of one
without the other. When psychotherapeutic work goes well, an individual
may move from concern about authoritarian approval, narcissistic sup-
plies, and involvement with oedipal objects into new freedom to be a self
with others. Time changes from passing moments of mere duration to an
opportunity to be (Ulanov, 1975, p.17). Saint Augustine called "time the
changing image of eternity." What meaning does eternity have for the
future of the self? This question is meant to evoke a background (perhaps
a dream screen) for the following reflections occasioned by rereading *The
Future of an Illusion* (Freud, 1928). There is indeed something peculiar
about the powerlessness of the intellect in comparison with the instinctual
life (p. 23). The powerlessness of the intellect in comparison with the
spiritual life seems to partake of that same peculiarity.

The experience of meaning and/or meaninglessness emerges out of the
depths of subjectivity-in-relation-to-reality. As ego and reality co-
constitute each other in infancy, subjectivity and meaning remain correla-
tive. The possibility of an exhaustive formulation of meaning would
presume an omniscient subject. We participate in a changing world of
meaning/meaninglessness both received and created. Our receptivity to
another person's answer to the question, "What is the meaning of life?",
changes in accord with how well their answer addresses the question,
"What is the meaning of *my* life?" We look for a reciprocal relation between articulation and lived experience; we look to the biography of the
person. If we are religious believers, we wish to attend to how the living
God is implicated in any response. If we are psychoanalytic thinkers, we
may wish to attend to the psychodynamics involved. If we are both, we
may make use of the perspectives of religious faith and psychoanalytic
thought to attend to any experience. Both perspectives can be used to
enrich, complement, replace, and/or compete (defensively or creatively)
with each other. Lived meaning/meaninglessness may serve as a correc-
tive to abstract theoretical formulations, theological or psychological.
Meaning/meaninglessness emerges from the living of life. From what
vantage point do we say to the subject, who may be ourselves, "Did you
create that answer or did you *find* it in the midst of life?" In *An Interrupted Life,* Etty Hillesum (1983) recalls finding meaning in the writing
of Rilke though her own conclusion was that his frail spirit might have
been crushed by the times she was living through. In the midst of the
holocaust, a young Jewess, soon to be murdered, articulates what it
means to be a Christian. "We must be willing to be a balm for all
wounds" (p. 196). Did she create that answer or did she find it in the
midst of life? Did she discover the living God?

Revisions are continually necessary in the complex interplay between
subjectivity and meaning. Post-Freud subjectivity without dreamlife is

unthinkable. Freud heroically used his genius to insist on the irrational-the-less-than-more-than-rational. Consciousness is never without the unconscious unless in madness. We remain ambivalent: "She's just dreaming": meaning: she is not realistic enough. "She's a dreamer": meaning: she is a creative thinker. Freud views religion as supporting perennial immaturity by providing an escape from harsh reality by contributing to wish-fulfilling illusions. Freud rejects religion as too close to magical illusions. His hope is in the future achievement of science. In our age when we are struggling not to be depersonalized or destroyed by our own technology, Freud's optimism regarding science seems anachronistic. His treatment of art makes his bias against religion stand out. Ironically, the Freudian opus places dream experience at the heart of subjectivity. It is thanks to Freud that the intermingling of inner and outer reality could be taken for granted by Winnicott (1965, 1971). Yet in the area of religion, Freud opted for resignation to what scientific mind, called Logos, a word evocative in connotations for believers in the Word, can discover about reality. Today "education to reality" includes inner psychic reality. Western Scriptures, too, placed a high value in interiority and traced the inward struggles of the believer in relation to a Presence—Transcendent Reality.

Transitional experiencing as described by Winnicott is not limited to infancy but is a realm of experiencing in and through which the subject comes to be (Eigen 1981). "We will never challenge the baby to elicit an answer to the question: did you create that or did you find it?" (Winnicott, 1971, p. 89). There are times in the course of therapy when the patient, like the baby, is not to be challenged. Illusions are a necessary part of psychic growth. Winnicott situated illusion in the realm of transitional experiencing. This realm is often reduced in meaning to a phase or tranquilizing part-object. Without the existence of this realm, of this potential space, the unfolding and discovery of subjectivity cannot take place. To attempt to rid the psyche of all illusions would be to rob the psyche of a vital means of becoming (Pontalis, 1981). The nonverification between reality and fantasy can aid the coming to be of the individual—of subjective meaning—in-process—through the creative and free play of individual and surround—whether that surround be a personal other, mother, father, God, institution, language, or culture. The intent of this paper is to demonstrate that illusions in the context of transitional experiencing may promote the further development of the self.

The open space of transitional experiencing preserves the paradox inherent in the intermingling of inner and outer reality and with it psychoanalytic as well as religious experience. A 24-year-old Catholic man soon to be married awakes from a nightmare of castration and annihilation. He is the son of an overbearing intrusive mother and a passive father whose reason he idealizes as wisdom. He clutches the cross he has hanging from his bedpost. He later describes with fetishistic pleasure the quality of the wood and the leather strap. He feels safer. According to Arieti (1981), "Idolatry is a form of response when something that is perceived as vague and abstract and therefore threatening . . . has to be concretized and made part of the material aspect of life" (p. 53). Therapy continues. The patient dreams of catching a dazzlingly beautiful fish. Is he symbolizing, undoing, mastering, denying? The Fort-da game comes to mind. Look what the wish does dealing with psychic pain. The idealized self as phallus is rescued from the undifferentiated maternal depths of the unconscious. The dream space reflects the transitional space within the transference or the transference within the transitional space. Instead of experiencing his felt powerlessness, this patient hallucinated the absence of his own penis and the presence of a maternal phallus. He glossed over his own experience; he failed to experience himself. As his therapist, I failed to match his illusion and thus facilitated the moment when the patient caught on and this time could experience what had been denied. In the interplay of past and present, the future—a new self-experience—emerged. As therapeutic disillusionment with his parents proceeded, the patient married, anticipated having children, and completed writing needed for higher education. This patient left behind his preoccupation with crosses as ornaments as a child leaves his or her teddy. He has been able to suffer his pain and forgive his parents. He does not talk about the cross as symbol. From my faith perspective he is ready to do so. Illusion is not necessarily an error. Disbelieving interpretations and proselytizing are equally out of place. If active maternal mirroring mediates higher organization in the baby by reflecting more than the infant self presents (Loewald, 1978, p. 15), might not the unarticulated faith of the therapist do the same?

Consider an unmarried female patient in her late 30s. She seems compliant in relation to her own despair. Deadness pervades the therapy room. After the painful end of a long sexual affair with a married man, she invests all her leisure time in church activities. She is reliable, available, considerate, and generous. She is praised by others as living the golden rule. Pursued by schizoid emptiness, she feels she would rather be dead. As her fear and hunger for others surface, so do her self-hate and envy. Others feel they have a right to live; she has always felt like a poisonous burden to others, especially her depressed mother with whom she lives. She begins to learn to say "no" to demands made on her. Her first real "no" sends her to sleep for the weekend but is part of a no-saying to stagnation and death. She begins a desperate struggle with envy. By this ever-so-small beginning of self-assertion, she opens the possibility of a future relation to value that is not subservient but clears the space for mutuality and, with that, love. Her narcissistic definition of her self as excluded from the realm of grace begins to weaken. "I think God loves me—I just don't feel it." Caught countertransferentially in her black-hole mother, I wonder how the thought ever came to her. Ironically, I recall Freud's description of his God, Logos, "the voice is a soft one but it does not rest until it has a gained a hearing—after a countless succession of rebuffs, it succeeds." Did I create it? Did I find it? My retrospective understanding of this moment as gift/grace obviously emerges from my faith perspective. My clinical judgment makes me wonder whether the patient wanted to find a way to protect me from her sense of Godforsakenness. I was saturated with a dreamlike sense of timelessness but not disconnected from the profound psychic lostness of the patient. Therapists too dwell in the realm of transitional experiencing.

Freud attacked religious ideas as contributing to static immaturity. His critique of religion as a transparent holding on to a dependent relation to exalted omnipotent parents for protection against the hardships of life is well known and well founded. This kind of religiosity is radically different from faith that sees the harsh realities and confronts suffering. Suffering may come as a narcissistic injury to all of us at some time but especially to those who feel their righteousness should protect them. Two patients who struggle with felt randomness and arbitrariness of fate (Providence?) come to mind. Sally is a woman in her late 20s whose parents are both dead. One parent died when she was a young child, the other recently. Sally approaches a confrontation with her bitterness regarding the death of her parents via displacement onto the, to her, arbitrary dismissal from a high-paying job because of office politics. "I couldn't believe that I could do my job and they could still let me go." She is beginning to recognize that she blanks out when she comes too close to feelings of sadness and rage. "Everything happens for a reason," she quotes the priest her mother confided in. Hoping to facilitate the free play of disillusionment/meaningless, I shrug my shoulders and say I don't know the reason. Clinging to illusion to deny what the self experiences becomes delusional. The search for causality may be part of any everyday paranoia that derives from treating the mind as God. Logos too can mask illusions and provide a deep source of resistance to change and personalization.

The other patient is a 20-year-old man who was driving a car at the time of an accident. The accident resulted in severe injuries to several passengers and a lawsuit against his father. Keith, a practicing Catholic, complains that he has a bitter gripe with God that this accident happened to him. He thinks of himself as theologically sophisticated and is surprised to hear himself complaining that God does not follow rules even though he gives them out. Keith's father is defensively hypercritical and this anthropomorphism, unbeknown to Keith, is a reflection of his experience of his father. Keith has informed me that when he feels good about himself for "charitable works" he feels as if there is no room for God. He also invites me to join in decrying his seduction by a homosexual priest. I decide to use this time to confront Keith with his own responsibility to take into account what he sees and to begin to process his disillusionment and rage. He is in danger of consolidating his identity around a sense of being victimized and this tragic (regardless of what part Keith's unconscious dynamics played) accident will be used to provide the alibi. He uses the failures of authority to avoid facing his fear of his own father and of his own becoming. My challenge makes Keith angry and he awaits our next session eagerly to let me know how angry he is. The anger he directs at me is that of a petulant child. We are clearly not in the arena of the outrage of Job-like faith.

Federn (1953) makes an important distinction between "suffering from a pain" and merely "feeling a pain." Suffering occurs when the pain is included within the ego's boundaries. "Everyone can recognize for himself, in his unavoidable reaction to painful experiences, the difference between feeling the pain and suffering it, between whether he lets the pain hurt from the outside, like an object, or from the inside, like a part of himself" (p. 268). The psychic work of mourning must replace the narcissistic "feeling a pain." Freud was right. When religious ideas are used to deny harsh reality they deplete the person; they also block the way to authentic faith. Suffering in this sense is integral to psychic and spiritual maturing. Here the paradox of a crucified God is relevant.

Impingement on the going-on being of the child, according to Winnicott (1965), produces a pathological division of the true and false self. *Infantile* is neither a morally derogatory category nor a reference to a reified past but to a layer of psychic life that perdures. Interpretations, often implicit invitations to see value, must be *timely* if they are not to induce the compliance which Winnicott so eloquently describes as a moral vacuum (p. 102). Values must be discovered and adhered to by a self that is nourished by, not subordinated to, such values. Received morality may serve as a barrier to psychic growth and personal discovery of values when moral adherence is expressive of subjective compliance or the rationalizations of unanalyzed superego functioning. Moral masochism/sadism reinforces depersonalization for the sake of the collectivity whether through religious or psychoanalytic institutions. Masochism often involves an evasion of personal life. All forms of tyranny—not only political—begin as a compensation for the failure of personal aliveness and the giving up of the subjective search for meaning. If psychoanalytic or religious teachings are imposed or assimilated in an authoritarian mode, the person—the subject—is diminished, even victimized, by those concepts and values that are meant to deepen and develop subjectivity. Conformity to psychoanalytic and religious concepts that lacks real depth may be unrecognized. Culture can and does function as a tryannical superego. In the psychoanalytic establishment certain cultural modes and tonalities are passed on along with the theory. Transmission of values via the superego may jeopardize development of individual subjectivity and encourage establishment thinking. Psychoanalytic training may begin to function like inauthentic religiosity and become a contradiction to itself. The final irony occurs when theory—education—replaces—becomes bigger than— the psychic reality of the subject. Primacy of the intellect may be a subtle/not-so-subtle form of tyranny.

REFERENCES

Arieti, S. (1981). *Abraham and the contemporary mind.* New York: Basic Books.
Eigen, M. (1981). The area of faith in Winnicott, Lacan, and Bion. *International Journal of Psychoanalysis, 62,* 413-433.
Federn, P. (1953). *Ego psychology and the psychoses.* London: Maresfield Reprints.
Hillesum, E. (1983). *An interrupted life.* New York: Pantheon.
Loewald, H. (1978). *Psychoanalysis and the history of the individual.* New Haven, CT: Yale University Press.
Loewald, H. (1980). *Papers on psychoanalysis.* New Haven, CT: Yale University Press.
Pontalis, J.B. (1977). *Frontiers in psychoanalysis between the dream and psychic pain.* New York: International Universities Press.
Ulanov, A. & Ulanov, B. (1975). *Religion and the unconscious.* Philadelphia, PA: The Westminster Press.
Winnicott, D. (1965). *The maturational processes and the facilitating environment.* New York: International Universities Press.
Winnicott, D. (1971). *Playing and reality.* New York: Basic Books.

The Spiritual Emergency Patient: Concept and Example

Steven J. Hendlin

The term "spiritual emergency" (Grof & Grof, 1981) grew from the recognition that many individuals experiencing episodes of non-ordinary states of consciousness accompanied by various emotional, perceptual, and psychosomatic manifestations were undergoing an evolutionary crisis rather than suffering from mental disease. The terms "transpersonal crisis" and "transformational crisis" have also been used to describe this phenomenon. Because traditional psychiatry has not recognized the difference between mystical and psychotic experiences (GAP Report, 1977), the mental health professional has not been taught to diagnose, understand, or treat the patient experiencing transpersonal crisis. And yet, it is becoming increasingly evident that, if properly understood and treated as difficult stages in a natural developmental process, spiritual emergencies can result in emotional and psychosomatic healing, creative problem solving, personality transformation, and conscious evolution. The term "spiritual emergency" suggests a crisis but also the potential for rising to a higher state of being. In a series of penetrating and comprehensive books, Wilber (1977, 1980, 1981) has discussed the principles of spectrum psychology and outlined the stages of transpersonal evolution on the individual and collective scale that provide a strong theoretical foundation for the spiritual emergency concept. Especially relevant has been his distinction between pre-egoic and trans-egoic states and the mistake in equating one with the other in traditional psychiatric views of mystical experience.

In viewing all unusual states of consciousness as pathological and attributing them to anatomical, physiological, and biochemical changes in the brain and to other medical causes, there has been no acknowledgment that any experiential states involving changes of consciousness could be potentially therapeutic and transformative. The traditional psychiatric approach has been the routine use of controlling and suppressive approaches to terminate such experiences. With the patient in transpersonal crisis, however, insensitive use of repressive measures can lead to chronicity

Steven Hendlin, PhD, is a clinical psychologist in the full-time private practice of psychotherapy in Tustin and Laguna Beach, California. He teaches humanistic and transpersonal psychology at the California Graduate Institute and is a student of Eastern philosophy.

and long-term dependence on tranquilizing medication or other psycho-active drugs with ensuing serious side effects and impoverishment of personality (an example would be the treatment given the uncle of the patient presented later in this article). It is therefore important to clarify theoretically the concept of transpersonal crisis and to develop comprehensive and effective approaches to their treatment (Grof & Grof, 1981, 1984; Hendlin, 1983a).

It has been found that spiritual emergencies can occur spontaneously without any precipitating factors, or can be triggered by emotional stress, physical exertion and stress, disease, accident, intense sexual experiences, childbirth, or exposure to psychedelic drugs. In many instances the catalyzing factor appears to be involvement in various meditative practices which are specifically designed to activate spiritual energies (see, for example, Krishna, 1970; Muktananda, 1974, 1979; Sanella, 1976; White, 1979; Woodroffe, 1964). The power of intensive meditation to alter perceptual, emotional, cognitive, and psychosomatic functioning of mental health professionals has also been documented (e.g., Hendlin, 1979, 1981; Kornfield, 1979; Shapiro, 1980; Walsh, 1977, 1978). As spiritual disciplines continue to gain popularity in the West, an increasing number of people are experiencing transpersonal crises that can be traced to their practice of Yoga, Zen, various movement meditations, *pranayama* (intense breathing exercises), *Kundalini* maneuvers, Tibetan Buddhist psychoenergetic exercises, and other forms of intense and focused self-exploration (for some of the problems that arise in thinking and practice, see Hendlin, 1983b).

RESEARCH SUPPORTING THE CONCEPT

Supportive evidence for the concept of spiritual emergency can be drawn from a variety of fields. Many traditions have developed deep understanding of evolutionary crises and sophisticated cartographies of their different steps. The general cross-cultural agreement about the value of these states is reflected in the fact that many ethnic groups have quite independently developed technologies to precipitate them for healing purposes (Grof & Grof, 1981, 1984). For example, the Kung, a primitive tribe in southern Africa's Kalahari Desert, are said to bring intense Kundalini, or energy experiences, through dancing until reaching ecstatic trance (Katz, 1982).

A classic source of knowledge in this area is the work of Jung (1960). His concepts of collective unconscious, archetypal dynamics, individuation, synchronicity, and others are important in the understanding of the psychotic process.

Other important influences on the concept of spiritual emergency include the founder of Psychosynthesis, Assagioli (1977), and the work by Bucke (1923), Laski (1968), and William James (1961). Maslow (1962) contributed to the theoretical foundations of transpersonal psychology in his focus on peak experiences in well-adapted individuals. He made it clear that mystical experience must not be confused with mental illness.

New approaches to psychosis have been offered by Laing (1965, 1967), Boisen (1962), Dabrowski (1966) and Van Dusen (1972, 1974). Grof's research (1976, 1980) of non-ordinary states of consciousness induced by psychedelics and non-drug techniques is important in alternative understanding of psychotic states. Also, Campbell's (1970) study of mythological forms is very relevant for the new approaches to spiritual crisis, particularly his description of the hero's journey that is directly applicable to the psychotic process.

The Jungian psychiatrist Perry (1974, 1976) made major practical and theoretical contributions to transpersonal crisis intervention. Silverman (1967, 1970, 1971) conducted basic laboratory research in schizophrenic patients and gained insights into the psychotic process and their perceptual style. The work of Perry and Silverman provided inspiration for an extensive clinical study that they conducted jointly with Rappaport (1978), exploring the possibilities of non-drug treatment of schizophrenia.

When the focus of the transpersonal crisis is on psychological death and rebirth, the resemblances between this process and inner experiences of the shamanic journey have been found to be striking (see, for example, Castaneda, 1968, 1971, 1973, 1974, 1977, 1981; Eliade, 1964; Harner, 1980).

TOWARD A DEFINITION

Certainly, not all experiences of unusual states of consciousness and intense perceptual, emotional, cognitive, and psychosomatic changes are "spiritual emergencies" or can be treated by the new strategies. A good medical and psychiatric examination is necessary to rule out brain dysfunction or diseases of other organs or systems of the body. It has been found that even some of those who have spiritual emergencies are inappropriate for the new approaches if they are unable to view their problems as *related to an inner process,* or are unwilling to undergo the pain of confronting the underlying experiences (Grof & Grof, 1984).

The medical considerations related to even purely psychological work include such issues as proper nutrition, supply of vitamins, adequate sleep and rest, and prevention of dehydration. Intense emotional work may have clear medical contraindications, for example, hyperventilation bringing on epileptic seizures.

The following are important criteria suggesting that a person might be experiencing a spiritual emergency and can be offered alternative treatment (Grof & Grof, 1984):

1. Episodes of unusual experiences which involve changes in consciousness and perceptual, emotional, cognitive, and psychosomatic functioning. There is a significant transpersonal emphasis in the person's process, such as dramatic death and rebirth sequences, mythological and archetypal phenomena, past incarnation memories, out-of-body experiences, incidence of synchronicities or extrasensory perception, indication of Kundalini awakening, states of mystical union, identification with cosmic consciousness, and others (see Grof, 1976).
2. Absence of an organic brain disorder underlying abnormal mental functioning, such as infection, tumor, cardiovascular or degenerative disease of the brain, and so forth.
3. Absence of a physical disease of another organ or system which is responsible for the mental disorder, such as uremia, diabetes, toxic states with delirium, and so forth.
4. Reasonably good general somatic and cardiovascular condition allowing the client to endure safely physical and emotional stress frequently associated with the experiential work and with the uncovering strategy.
5. The ability to see the condition as an inner psychological process and to approach it in an internalized way. The capacity to form an adequate working therapeutic relationship and maintain the spirit of cooperation. This excludes persons with severe paranoid states, persecutory delusions and hallucinations who use consistently the mechanisms of projection, externalization, and acting out.
6. Absence of a long history of conventional psychiatric treatment and hospitalizations which generally tend to make the application of the new approaches much more difficult or impossible.
7. Since it is not possible in some cases to draw a clear line between spiritual emergency and psychosis, it might be necessary to postpone the final decision about the strategy of treatment until the response of the client to the new techniques has been tested experimentally.

CLINICAL EXAMPLE OF SPIRITUAL EMERGENCY

Background: History, Symptoms, and Relevant Data

Robert, 32, was referred to me through the Spiritual Emergency Network at Esalen Institute. He was looking for a therapist who would be understanding of and sympathetic to the spiritual crisis he had been struggling with for some time. He had been moderately depressed for the last 6 months since having intense physical, perceptual, and spiritual experiences as a result of individual and group meditations associated with joining a spiritual group in which he had been active for 3 years. Psychosocial stressors included marital difficulties as a result of his wife's strong feelings against his group participation, which meant much time away from her and his children; and a falling out with two business partners (who were also mentors), which cost him friendships and created financial problems. Robert had been meditating for almost 5 years. His meditation consisted of a spiral visualization in which energy was moved up various centers of the body, culminating in white light "blissing out" at the crown of the head. He would periodically fast, frequently attended weekend, week-long, or longer retreats, and was strongly attached to and idealizing of his spiritual teacher, who was grooming him to become a leader of group energy workshops. These workshops included group energy sharing through hands-on methods which could be powerful in evoking emotional, psychological, physical, and spiritual experiences in participants.

Robert presented as severely depressed with suicidal ideation, complaining of poor sleep and strong currents of energy through his body, especially in the head area. He heard a constant buzzing in his ears which he couldn't turn off. He felt he did not want to live unless he could reduce this energy, that it would drive him crazy. He reported many positive and negative emotional, perceptual, and physical experiences, all of which were framed within a spiritual context. He had been prescribed Atapin, a mood elevator, by a psychiatrist he had consulted shortly before initiating contact with me.

Important background data included the following: Robert's father had pursued a spiritual path his whole life and was mostly in the background in Robert's growing up. Meditating, writing books on spiritual topics, and producing intricate graphics with spiritual themes, his father had been revered by Robert as a "father-saint" who was mostly quiet, passive, and undemanding of Robert and his two younger brothers. His father left most of the child-rearing to Robert's mother, who was actively involved in her own career as an art teacher. Shortly after divorcing Robert's mother, his father was killed in an automobile accident. There was some question as to whether the accident was an intentional suicide, as his father had been quite depressed after the divorce. His death precipitated a spiritual searching undertaken by Robert, his mother, and two brothers.

An uncle had experienced a "nervous breakdown" in his 30s and was never able to recover, requiring ongoing psychotropic medication, and was unable to work through his life. His breakdown was apparently associated with exploring spiritual practices along with Robert's father. Robert feared ending up like his uncle and had a terrifying dream which he took to be a premonition 2 weeks before our initial contact. In his own words:

> I dreamed I was on a sailboat with my two young children and as we cast off from shore, I realized my uncle was the captain. It was a beautiful day and no sooner had we left the land than he said he was not sure what to do. He then made a sailing mistake and my two children were cast overboard. The oldest one could swim and he hung on to the back of the boat but the little one fell straight to the bottom. I dove down to the bottom to rescue him and brought him to the surface just in time. (As I'm writing this I'm feeling that this was the "newborn" me, who had fallen so deep and was rescued just in time.) I had never given my uncle's reality a thought in my life but now the pain of seeing that I could become my uncle drove me into a panic state of unsureness and misconception. Death seemed like the only answer to deal with this intense pain. I actually climbed a cliff behind the retreat building for 3 straight days and peered over the cliff. I really wanted to jump but for some reason some part of me wouldn't let go.

Robert believed there might be a family "curse" which brought the demise of all family members who went "too far out" in their attempts to attain mystical states of consciousness. A sense of guilt over "defying the Gods" pervaded his recounting of his spiritual experiences under his teacher.

As mentioned, Robert was being groomed to lead workshops himself, even though he had no training except having been a participant. As he began organizing weekend retreats, he would experience bouts of depression and physical illness just before he was to lead a group. Rather than pay attention to this sign that something was wrong, he would instead "cleanse" himself through meditation and "transcend" the feelings of depression and physical illness through intense energy exchanges with group participants. At no time did Robert question the judgment of his teacher, who, although well meaning, was not trained as a mental health professional and did not know his own limits in dealing with Robert's need for help. His teacher considered these difficulties as unpleasant but unavoidable side effects of spiritual evolution, which, although partially true, did not help Robert deal with the intense pain and suicidal feelings he was experiencing. It is not insignificant that his teacher was trained as a physician and thus should have been familiar with the need for referral to a competent therapist.

Treatment

It was apparent to me that Robert was in a crisis. We met four times the first week with added phone contacts. Hospitalization was not desired nor did it seem necessary. The second week we met three times and continued three times weekly contact until the 33rd hour at which time we cut back to twice weekly. The working diagnosis given was *major depressive episode with melancholia.* Treatment initially consisted of supportive listening to his experiences, reassurance that we could deal with his pain together, and gaining Robert's trust after his being let down by his teacher. While supporting Robert's framing of issues within a spiritual context, I made it clear to him that I believed basic *psychological-developmental* issues had been neglected which were now causing great conflict and which needed attention.

As Robert began to trust me, we began to examine his anger and resentment toward his teacher for not being able to handle him more appropriately. It took some time for him to go beyond his idealization of his teacher and to own his negative feelings that up to this point had been denied or rationalized away. Robert was also given at the fourth session a basic grounding meditation to help him redirect the energy in the head area which was responsible for his sense of "bursting." He was advised to pay attention to his feet touching the ground as he walked and to follow his breathing at his abdomen as he sat quietly with his eyes *open* (to prevent spacing out). By the sixth hour he was feeling stronger and getting some sleep and by the 15th hour we began to experiment with cutting back his medication, which he did after informing his psychiatrist. The abdomen breathing meditation included counting the breaths upon exhalation, which was used to further help focus attention and ground energy in the abdomen area. The important aspect of my initial work with Robert was in valuing his spiritual experiences *without having to accept his way of interpreting them.* I could see that he would not allow me to work with him on psychodynamic issues which had precipitated his crisis until he trusted that I understood the importance of his experiences and the meaning of his spiritual quest. So, I could relate to his search to find "oneness" with God *and* I could see he also was trying to become "one" with his father.

Robert didn't know if he was a "saint" or a "sinner." As our work progressed he came to see how the use of altered states of consciousness helped cover up more basic ego-level concerns. I supported Robert's experiences by inviting him to share with me graphics he had produced (like his father) that reflected perceptions from altered states. We worked with dreams which contained spiritually symbolic material as well as messages regarding fears and hopes for recovery. Issues which emerged in our work included passive-aggressive behavior with his wife, unfinished business with both father and mother, and a difficulty in letting himself feel angry with anyone, because to allow this would be to move out of the "heart space" which called for unconditional Christlike love no matter what may occur in relationships with friends, in business, and so forth. He also came to accept other impulses, such as his sexuality, which for some time had been viewed as "anti-spiritual" and part of one's "lower" nature.

After 4 months of treatment Robert discontinued use of all medication and felt significantly stronger, with less fear and fewer episodes of insomnia. His ability to handle small amounts of stress from his hectic business increased and he began to get involved caring for his children, including most of the housework while his wife helped manage their business. After about 100 hours, we began marital therapy to deal with relationship problems caused by many years of distance between Robert and his wife and brought to a head by his crisis.

Continuing to grow stronger, Robert is learning how to create a spiritual practice within the context of his ongoing family life and has, after some struggle, given up his fantasy of being an adored spiritual teacher. He is attempting to create projects which will satisfy his need to find meaning in helping people in a way his retail business does not provide. He has no desire to see his teacher again or to return to the spiritual group although he does desire contact with others who have been through similar spiritual experiences in hopes of better understanding what happened to him.

DISCUSSION AND FINAL COMMENTS

Robert's spiritual crisis was of a fairly typical nature: after intensive spiritual practices, physical, emotional, and perceptual experiences, which can no longer be understood within the spiritual framework in which they are presented, begin to have a devastating effect and lead to severe depression and suicidal ideation. Dealing with the consequences of awakened energy in the body becomes an all-consuming preoccupation. In treating Robert, I listen supportively to and am accepting of their significance to him without in any way labeling them "pathological." I help Robert re-cast them into identifiable and manageable psychological terms. In asking him to try a different form of meditation than he was used to, I take advantage of a skill he has already learned in order to help him ground himself rather than to "bliss out." I focus with him on significant relationships which have been neglected but which are vital to his understanding of the "path" he has pursued. As Robert's discriminating mind is developed, he is able to see that he was a victim of "group-think" and that he will have to learn to trust *himself* more in creating his life and stay in touch with the part of him which is looking for a wise father-figure to lead him to *nirvana*. The previous split caused by seeking the spiritual at any cost becomes tempered by the desire to re-own his family and to carve his spiritual path in the daily "marketplace."

The spiritual emergency patient is an emerging phenomenon of our times, not unlike the borderline and narcissistic personality disorders. If we are to address the needs of these patients we will have to respect healthy spiritual seeking, understand the pitfalls along the way, depathologize this healthy seeking, and act as "existential guides" who have, in some way, been there and returned unscathed. Although not a role for all psychotherapists, it will attract those who value the spiritual in their own lives and who choose not to collapse altered states of consciousness into a pathological nosology.

REFERENCES

Assagioli, R. (1977). Self-regulation and psychological disturbances. *Synthesis, 3-4.*

Boisen A. (1962). *The exploration of the inner world.* New York: Harper & Row.

Bucke, R. (1923). *Cosmic consciousness.* New York: Dutton.

Campbell, J. (1970). *Hero with a thousand faces.* Cleveland: World Publishing Co.

Castaneda, C. (1968). *Teachings of Don Juan: A Yaqui way of knowledge.* Berkeley: University of California Press.

Castaneda, C. (1971). *A separate reality: Further conversations with Don Juan.* New York: Simon & Schuster.

Castaneda, C. (1973). *Journey to Ixtlan: The lessons of Don Juan.* New York: Simon & Schuster.

Castaneda, C. (1977). *The second ring of power.* New York: Simon & Schuster.

Castaneda, C. (1974). *Tales of power.* New York: Simon & Schuster.

Castaneda, C. (1981). *The eagle's gift.* New York: Simon & Schuster.

Dabrowski, K. (1966). *Positive disintegration.* Boston: Little, Brown.

Eliade, M. (1964). *Shamanism: The archaic techniques of ecstasy.* New York: Pantheon.

Grof, S. (1976) *Realms of the human unconscious: Observations from LSD research.* New York: Dutton.

Grof, S. (1980). *LSD psychotherapy.* Pomona: Hunter House.

Grof, C. & Grof, S. (1981, June). *Spiritual Emergency Newsletter, 1*(1).

Grof, C. & Grof, S. (1984, January). Spiritual emergency: Understanding and treatment of transpersonal crises. *Spiritual Emergency Network Newsletter.*

Group for the Advancement of Psychiatry. (1977) *Mysticism: spiritual quest or psychic disorder?* Washington, DC: Group for the Advancement of Psychiatry.

Harner, M. (1980) *The way of the Shaman.* New York: Harper & Row.

Hendlin, S. (1979) Initial Zen intensive (sesshin): A subjective account. *Journal of Pastoral Counseling, 14*(2), 27-43.

Hendlin, S. (1981). Every second at just the right time: A tale of intensive Zen practice. *Pilgrimage, 9*(1), 39-47.

Hendlin, S. (1983a). *Spiritual emergency: A clinical case study.* Paper presented to Eleventh Annual Conference of the Association for Transpersonal Psychology, Asilomar, June.

Hendlin, S. (1983b). Pernicious oneness. *Journal of Humanistic Psychology, 23*(3), 61-81.

James, W. (1961). *Varieties of religious experience.* New York: Collier.

Jung, C. G. (1960). *Collected works.* Bollingen Series XX, Princeton, NJ: Princeton University Press.

Katz, R. (1982) *Boiling energy: Community healing among the Kalahori Kung.* Cambridge: Harvard University Press.

Kornfield, J. (1979) Intensive insight meditation: A phenomenological study. *Journal of Transpersonal Psychology, 11*(1), 41-58.

Krishna, G. (1970). *Kundalini: The evolutionary energy in man.* Berkeley: Shambhala.

Laing, R. D. (1965). *The divided self.* Baltimore: Penguin.

Laing, R. D. (1967). *The politics of experience.* New York: Ballentine.

Laski, M. (1968). *Ecstacy: A study of some secular and religious experiences.* New York: Greenwood Press.

Maslow, A. (1962). *Toward a psychology of being.* Princeton, NJ: Van Nostrand.

Muktananda, Swami (1974). *Play of consciousness.* South Fallsberg, NY: SYDA Foundation.

Muktananda, Swami (1979). *Kundalini: The secret of life.* South Fallsberg, NY: SYDA Foundation.

Perry, J. (1974). *The far side of madness.* Englewood Cliffs, NJ: Prentice-Hall.

Perry, J. (1976) *Roots of renewal in myth and madness.* San Francisco: Jossey-Bass.

Rappaport, M. et al. (1978). Are there schizophrenics for whom drugs may be unnecessary or con-traindicated? *International Pharmacopsychiatry, 13,* 100.

Sanella, L. (1976). *Kundalini: Psychosis or transcendence?* San Francisco: H.R. Dakin.

Shapiro, D.H. (1980) *Meditation: Self-regulation strategy and altered states of consciousness.* New York: Aldine.

Silverman, J. (1967). Shamans and acute schizophrenia. *American Anthropologist, 69,* 21.

Silverman, J. (1970). Acute schizophrenia: Disease or dis-ease? *Psychology Today, 4,* p. 64.

Silverman, J. (1971, October). When schizophrenia helps. *Psychology Today.*

Van Dusen, W. (1972). *The natural depth in man.* New York: Harper & Row.

Van Dusen, W. (1974). *The presence of other worlds: The teachings of Emanuel Swedenborg.* New York: Harper & Row.

Walsh, R. (1977). Initial meditative experiences: I. *Journal of Transpersonal Psychology, 9*(2), 151-192.

Walsh, R. (1978) Initial meditative experiences: II. *Journal of Transpersonal Psychology, 10*(1), 1-28.

White, J. (Ed.) (1979). *Kundalini, evolution and enlightenment.* Garden City, NY: Anchor Books.

Wilber, K. (1977). *The spectrum of consciousness.* Wheaton, IL: Theosophical Publishing House.

Wilber, K. (1980). *The Atman project: A transpersonal view of human development.* Wheaton, IL: Theosophical Publishing House.

Wilber, K. (1981). *Up from Eden: A transpersonal view of human evolution.* New York: Doubleday.

Woodroffe, Sir J. (1964). *The serpent power.* Madras: Ganesh.

Formation Counseling

Adrian van Kaam

Formation counseling is one of the main applications of the science of distinctively human or spiritual formation. It awakens and sustains in counselees the art and discipline of formative apprehension and appraisal. This type of appraisal relates directly to their actual life formation. People who come to counselors with the normal problems of consonant form reception and donation in our culture do not necessarily have to be referred to intensive psychotherapeutic treatment. They may be helped by formation counseling, which draws upon the insights and findings of the science of formation. This science in turn integrates the relevant contributions of the arts and sciences with the wisdom of the great formation traditions of humanity. This does not mean that certain principles of formation counseling could not be relevant to or for psychotherapy.

FORMATIVE APPREHENSION AND APPRAISAL

One of the problems of counselees in our culture is that they are accustomed mainly to informative thinking. They lost or never acquired the art of formative apprehension and appraisal fostered in the great formation traditions of humanity.

Counselees have to realize that they are always receiving or giving form in their lives, be it usually in a prefocal or unfocused fashion. In the counseling sessions they learn to focus on this process in a way that is primarily formative instead of informative. They become aware that many experiences manifest and foster this formation process, but that they are inclined to deny these experiences, to bypass them as insignificant, or to use them merely as neutral matter for informative thinking.

Formation counseling assists them in the disclosure of the unique meaning of their experiences for their formation. It enables them to gain insight into the structures, dimensions, conditions, and dynamics of their

Adrian van Kaam, CSSp, was born in Holland where he later joined the Congregation of the Holy Spirit and was ordained a priest. He received his PhD in psychology from Western Reserve University in Cleveland. He is founder and director emeritus of the Institute of Formative Spirituality at Duquesne University where he is professor of foundational formation. Father van Kaam is editor of the journal, *Studies in Formative Spirituality,* and of *Envoy.* He is an internationally known lecturer and author of over 25 books and numerous articles in national and international publications.

89

formation process, its consonant and dissonant directions. This type of counseling creates space for an enlightened dwelling on their experiences in order to appraise them as helpful or harmful for consonant human unfolding. Gradually counselees come to see that their excessive dependence on informative-functional thought is not sufficient for the full flowering of their life. It should be balanced by formative reflection as the gentle master of human existence.

Until now, formative thinking has been represented for the most part by spiritual masters in the East and West. The science of formation integrates their insights with the relevant contributions of the arts and sciences that emerged more recently in history. The science itself and the formation counseling sessions it fosters, either in common or in private, highlight humanity's primary tendency to give and to receive form in life and world in relative freedom together with others. These sessions bring into the open the obstacles and facilitating conditions the counselees meet on this journey, the ever-present threat of deformation, the ability to cope with it effectively.

EMERGENCE OF THE NEED FOR FORMATION COUNSELING

At times in our life, a congenial and compatible form of existence seems to emerge almost effortlessly. Formative inspirations, aspirations, ambitions, pulsions, and pulsations arise spontaneously in natural consonance with one another. We sense that we are growing wisely and graciously. We feel in harmony with the world. Life flows easily. Formation is not problematic.

At other moments, however, we may feel compelled to think about what happens to us in our formation. Often we are brought to reflection by some crisis that interrupts the spontaneous flow of life, or by a conflict that disrupts our daily routine. These problems may continue because we do not know how to solve the tension between the spontaneous formation of our life and the formative reflection that should guide it at moments of decisive re-direction. We may have lost contact with the great formation traditions of humanity, which could awaken this formative wisdom. Neither is this wisdom made available to us in a living way by theological propositions or psychological theories, if these are not illumined by the age-old treasure of human formation experience. Hence, we may have to turn to formation counseling to receive the light needed for the solution of such normal problems of growth in contemporary humanity.

Such counseling sessions help us to question the sense of the situations we are facing. What do these formation events really mean for us? We begin to ask ourselves how we may foster consonant formation. Can we do something about it by means of meditative reflection or recourse to formation wisdom and tradition; to formative reading; to the exercise of formative apprehension, appraisal, affirmation, and other means of disclosing consonant form directives? Counselees begin to feel increasingly the need to appraise who they are and where they are going. The moment they begin to reflect on their formation experience, they initiate the possibility of critically appraising their life direction.

FORMATION FIELD

The human life form is always involved in a field of formation. This field is the totality of all the factors that have a formative impact on a person's inner and outer life. The life of our counselees is interwoven with this field. They live in it as an oyster in its shell, a fish in its pond, a fetus in the womb. The human form of life is always in ongoing formation, but only in and through its formation field. Each human life form, and each community of human forms, develops its own field through unique dialogue.

For example, the field in which our American counselees give form to their life differs from that of the Indians, Bantus, or Eskimos. Things have a different formative meaning for them. Even if the information about these things is the same, their *formative meaning,* the real difference they make in one's spiritual, functional, vital, and sociohistorical life may be quite different. The fact that all people over the globe are increasingly participating in the same information about things makes us too easily assume that they have the same formative impact on them. This is not necessarily the case. For instance, African converts to Islam or Christianity may be informed about the tenets of their new religion. Yet its formative impact will be modulated, subtly and usually prefocally, by the interiorized formative meanings of their tribal traditional formation field. Briefly, formation fields are not the same for people of different periods and cultures.

The animal form of life, on the other hand, seems to maintain basically the same type of formation field. Hence, we do not see much change in patterns of building shelter, mating behavior, or ways of rearing young. However, we are changing all the time ways in which we receive and give form in our field. We dress in new fashions, cultivate the earth with new machines, differentiate our sciences into ever more refined ones, create new forms of aesthetic expression, soar off into space. The human life form does not seem as bound to a naturally inherited formation field as that of animals. In some way we keep giving form to our own field. We cannot realize our own form potencies without giving form to the very potencies of the field in which we live. In short, we form ourselves by forming our field. We are people in constant reformation.

For example, we formed ourselves as city dwellers by building cities, as industrialists by developing mills and plants. We became readers by printing books; travelers by giving form to trains, cars and planes; astronauts by producing space crafts and satellites.

Our formation field is the domain of our form potencies. They are ours in and through this field. Without our formation field, we would be nothing potentially. We experiment with our formation field in innumerable ways because this is our only road to ongoing formation. Each time we are formatively in touch with our formation field in a new manner, we receive or give form to a new mode of our humanity. When we probe our field, we actualize our form potency for empirical investigation; when we care for people we grow in love; when we admire the beauty of nature our aesthetic sense is formed in depth. When we dig a hole, chop down a tree, fly a kite, or prepare a new dish, we are formed in practical insight, aptitude, and agility. In short, we are formed humanly by our manifold formative engagement in our fields of action and contemplation.

FORM POTENCIES

A human form potency is thus a dynamic tendency striving to give or receive form. Definite form potencies permeate the life form of our counselees; their apprehensions, appraisals, and affirmations of their formation field; their actions and apparent behavior. Counselees may be oblivious to the pressure of denied potencies. Such awareness is due to repudiation or to a refusal of the call inherent in their form potencies. This lack of awareness leads inevitably to disturbance. The relief of such disturbance presupposes that one face the denied potency and its urgent call. It does not necessarily mean that a person will realize this invitation. A free and insightful decision to forego a certain formation possibility in favor of another can be healthy and invigorating, provided this option ties in with an overall consonant project of life that makes sense to a person here and now at this juncture of one's formation history.

Our counselees cannot find consonance of life as long as they repudiate or refuse to face their emergent form potencies. They must come to terms with them realistically in accordance with their formation field as apprehended and appraised in the light of their freely chosen formation traditions.

POWER OF EMERGENT FORMATION POTENCIES

The emergence of a form potency implies a powerful motive to give or to receive form accordingly. For example, at a certain age children experience a challenge to give new form to their movements in the playpen.

Their formation field becomes structured momentarily around this awakening of their form potency. Their field becomes different in the light of this potency, which presses for a new modulation of their bodily form. In their field the open arms of inviting and encouraging parents appear as a harbor to which they can safely travel; chairs become instruments to lean upon in their first awkward attempts to new form donation; belts with which they are bound are resented as obstacles to formation.

Later on in life, we may apprehend and appraise similar reformations of our field when challenged by other emergent potencies. Consider the field of the adolescent who experiences the first stirrings of love, of executives who sense that they could reach the top, of scholars or artists who feel they may achieve something great in their field. At such moments other form potencies seem to recede in the background, at least temporarily. The human form involved in such an emergent tendency is mainly aware of what may lead to the desired form of life and achievement.

Ultimately, it is our transcendent personal choice that should freely decide what kinds of form donation and reception should receive priority. We should not allow ourselves to be overcome by the pressure of emergent form potencies. Prefocally, mutually incompatible kinds of potencies may dominate our actions; we become confused and erratic, irrational and tense. Our formation journey is no longer smooth and even. A great deal of formation counseling is taken up with making these prefocal pressures of emergent form potencies focal and in assisting the counselees to decide on their priorities in the light of the ideological or religious formation traditions to which they have freely committed themselves. The latter imply necessarily that they become aware of what these implicit secular or religious traditions mean for them, formatively speaking.

We conclude that a human form potency is a focal or prefocal (in some instances, an infra or transfocal) dynamic tendency toward a specific form reception or donation in one's formation field. As a motivating force, it colors one's apprehension, appreciation, and affirmation. Which particular form potencies gain priority in our life depends to a large extent on our prefocal hierarchy of form potencies. This heirarchy is formed under the influence of one's formation history, one's formation phase, innate affinities, form traditions, and personal affirmations. Many, if not all of these forming influences, may enter into the dialogue of formation counseling.

FORMATION COUNSELING AS SUCH

Formation counseling is essentially a process of making people free for their own formation. They come to us because, under the average pressures of deformative accretions and pulsations of some of their form traditions, they have lost their formation freedom in certain sectors of life. They can no longer transcend the formative directives imposed by sociohistorical pulsations in their formation field. They have repudiated or refused to allow emergent form potencies to come into awareness. This repudiation is embodied in dissonant reactions and responses. These may be extinguished gradually after gaining insight during the counseling sessions in their inhibitory power. They may be replaced by the conditioning of other responses generated by new consonant form directives. The latter should correspond to a new, more free apprehension, appraisal, and affirmation of their formation field.

Counselees can be known from their unique field of formation, not from an isolated and interior intrasphere. Therefore, from the very beginning, the formation counselor orients the attention of the counselees toward themselves as receiving and giving form in their unique field of self, people, events, and things in the light of the formation mystery. They are encouraged not to escape their ongoing formation by a flight into the past, where there are no decisions to make and where there is no necessity to reform freely the present field of form reception and donation, where one's life form seems explained and justified by inescapable determinants. Instead of forcing counselees to revise the fixed form history of their past, they are invited to face their formation field today, not to excuse themselves but to realistically confront their actual field of life in a new mode of presence, to accept its challenges. Past formation history will only be referred to in service of a clarification of the challenges of the present.

The aim of formation counseling is to make the counselees feel at home in their real field by reforming their unrealistic apprehensions, appraisals, affirmations, aspirations, ambitions, pulsions, and pulsations. Transcending the barriers to free formation, they learn how to move with a new freedom and consonance in daily life. Only people who can call their real field their dwelling place can cope with formation anxiety. They accept and affirm their whole field, not only its bright but its dark side as well.

FORMATIVE DISPOSITIONS AND EXPRESSIONS

Formation counselors translate these objectives into appropriate dispositions which are in turn embodied in word, posture, facial expression, and bodily movement. Such dispositions and expressions are formed in the light of the purpose of formation counseling as well as of the formation field of the counselees. *Their* modes of forming apprehension, appraisal, and affirmation must be clarified. *Their* personal field of presence has to be explored and expressed by means of counseling relationship. To sense which dispositions and expressions of ours may give effective form to our directives for specific counselees, we should gradually gain an appreciation of *their* field of formation. Subsequently, we will grow during the sessions into the right appraisal of the kinds of relationships which may induce our counselees to explore and express their field and their formation projects in the light of the form traditions to which they have implicitly or explicitly committed themselves. Such crucial commitment itself will often be the focus of shared exploration.

FORMATION PROJECT

As mentioned earlier, the main characteristic of the human form of life is its ongoing formation by means of a succession of current formation projects. These are tentative answers to its unfolding formation field. The feelings, desires, hopes, and ideas; the imaginations, memories, and anticipations of counselees are embedded in such projects, usually prefocally. They form together a system of formation directives. Every directive that becomes the focus of our shared exploration has a place somewhere in this system. It sheds light on all other directives.

The structure of a formation project as a differentiated whole explains partly the formative power and orientation of every single directive which participates in it. Each directive in turn colors all directives which make up the current formation project of the counselee. Counselees are gradually able to apprehend and to express the main lines of their current formation project. As formation anxiety diminishes, they may finally see and appraise the deformative impact of dissonant directives within this system. On the basis of this appraisal, they may be ready to develop a new current formation project more congenial with who they are as a unique constellation of form potencies and more compatible with their actual formation field here and how, including the traditions to which they are committed.

INTERFORMATIVE RELATIONSHIP

The interformative relationship between counselor and counselee is the principal means for bringing to expression the formation project which the counselee currently lives. The quality of the interformative relationship influences to what degree one's project of formation as well as one's personal field will find adequate expression. The counselor establishes a relationship which leads to diminishment of formation anxiety and to optimal communication.

People learn to hide their personal formation projects in order to protect themselves, by means of security directives, from being misunder-

stood, humiliated, ridiculed, condemned, or abused. To disclose their
personal project is in a sense to surrender their life form, to expose their
sensitivity, and to unveil their vulnerability when certain directives which
they cherish are at odds with the form directives appreciated by their environment. Fear of disapproval and depreciation limits the free admission
not only of base inclinations but also of sublime aspirations. It is difficult
for many to verbalize their finer sentiments. They fear that the communication or refined feelings would sound ridiculous in the field of one-sided
functionalistic appreciation shared with their contemporaries.

This refusal of higher aspirations under the pressure of a shared functionalistic field of action may be terribly effective. Counselees themselves
may not be aware of the deepest personal aspirations at the root of their
preformed life, crying out for expression in their empirical life form.
Counselors may make themselves mistakenly the allies of this sociohistorical, functionalistic field. They may joke lightly about "noble sentiments"
in order to reassure *apparently* functionalistic counselees that they are
"regular fellows" like the rest of the population. As a result, the hidden
aspirations of their counselees may remain a closed book. Some counselors may cherish the illusion that such "open-mindedness" breaks
down barriers. They forget that an exclusive openness to the contemporary scene may mean closure to the denied personal aspirations of the
counselee.

IMPOSITION OF ONE'S OWN FORM OF LIFE

Every one of us has an own current project of formation. This implies,
among other things, the formation traditions in accordance with which we
embody our strivings in everyday formative efforts. Such form traditions
have been absorbed via the dispositions and expressions of the culture in
which we are inserted by birth and initial formation. Our form traditions
permeate our interformative relationships with others. This connection is
particularly pervasive in the encounter between us as counselors and the
counselees who come to us for the facilitation of their formation journey.
The subtle influence of our own form traditions could be confusing. Our
personal embodiment of life formation is not the only possible or desirable one for others. The identification of our own formation project as
"the" project for all may limit our relevance to that segment of the population which is spontaneously in touch with our own traditions and our
personal version of them. At the same time, we risk repelling others who
are not similarly disposed.

Therefore, counselors should grow increasingly in the appraisal of
their own dispositions. Of course, they cannot do away with a personal
form of life. They must embody their presence in some apparent expres-

sion, which is, of necessity, limited in time and space and, therefore, necessarily one-sided. But they can increasingly free themselves from the identification of consonant human formation as such with their own formation project. This inner freedom will enable them to sense the unique form potencies, form directives, and formation field of those who differ from them.

Formation counselors should be aware of the impact of their own traditions, their cultural and subcultural stereotypes, their antipathies and sympathies, their affinities. Emotional blocks will become manifest to them in this maturity. They may disclose, for instance, that they feel uneasy with people who have aesthetic inclinations because the folks at home confused artistry with frivolity. Such confusion may be traced to a historical overreactive rejection of all art and beauty because of the danger of an idolizing of secular aestheticism during a certain cultural period. This threat may have generated a deformative accretion of their formation tradition. Such dissonant accretions, if not worked through, render counselors less effective and unnecessarily inhibiting in their formative presence.

Other counselors may realize that they one-sidedly prefer "regular guys" because as high school or college students they disliked some companions who were delighted more by books than by baseballs. Some, on the contrary, may find that they are enamored with scholarly types because they are fed up with more pragmatic colleagues who make fun of them.

Certain counselors again may discover during this process of ongoing formation that they lean toward compulsiveness because they have identified the compulsive form of life with sound discipline and firmness. Hence, they distrust spontaneity in themselves and in their counselees.

FORMATION COUNSELOR AND FORMATION TRADITIONS

Formation happens from infancy on. It may start already in the fetal stage of life. It is influenced by our interformative interaction with our parents or guardians. They communicate to us in words, gestures, and actions what people in their secular and/or religious traditions appraise as advantageous in the formation of acts and dispositions. Our initial life orientation is not fashioned in isolation but in dialogue with the life-style of representatives of one or more form traditions.

It is thus not so that children develop their formation project with a wary eye on their real form potencies. Children are not faced with the ideal directives of formation as such, but with their parents' appraisal of desirable life formation. The parents' appraisal is coformed in turn by the view of formation that prevails in their traditions. No human life form is an island in the great sea of formation. Directives are deeply interwoven with the interests of humanity and of each human community in their formation history.

To be sure, we ought to assimilate the directives of form traditions in a unique and congenial way. They should really become ours in the course of our formation history. The basic directives of the great classical traditions are not ordinarily contrary to the givenness of the human form in its fundamental dimensions and articulations. They are the fruit of revered wisdom, revelation, and the experiences of generations. The sober core of such age-old wisdom is usually consonant with at least the main foundations of human life. This wisdom, however, is incorporated in directives, dispositions, and customs which change with historical situations. Its adaptive embodiment in concrete styles of life may be at odds with what we foundationally are called to be by the formation mystery. These concrete expressions of form traditions are dictated not only by the foundations of the vision of generations. They are influenced also by the temporal or regional demands of the changing situations in which this vision has to be realized.

Our counselees often confuse the core of the accumulated wisdom of their form traditions with its historical accretions, some of which may be dissonant and deformative. They may represent safeguards or secondary security directives. Our counselees may have made them ends in themselves. Safeguards have perhaps taken the place of the directives they were designed to protect. They take on a life of their own. Their growth is no longer rooted in the fundamental directives of their traditions; rather they loom up as isolated powers. Thus the myriad safeguards developed over the centuries may have become for some counselees a stern police force hemming in their distinctively human formation. Safety directives may have become excessive in extent and intensity. They may even contradict the very directives they were meant to protect.

Formation counselors should carefully watch their own prefocal dispositions. They should not depreciate the consonant foundations of the tradition to which their counselees have committed themselves in their style of formation. They should help people to clarify the formation potential of the tradition they have chosen and encourage the unique way in which persons try to implement such foundations.

Formation counselors ought to distinguish between the truly fundamental and the merely personal in their appraisal. They may discover that certain people live the directives of their tradition in an unwholesome, overanxious fashion that elicits dissonant dispositions and actions. Inexperienced or uninformed counselors may identify this unhealthy expression with the directives themselves. They may be appalled by the deforming consequences. Implicitly or explicitly, counselors may then communicate that they themselves do not appreciate the fundamental directives of the traditions of the counselees. By doing so they may drain away the motivating and integrating power of the traditional infrastructure of a person's life. However, it is in the light of this traditional introjected structure that counselees may eventually be able to integrate their life formation more wholesomely with the entire formation field. Outside their form tradition they may lose their possibility for consonant integration. It may be replaced by the opposite of integration, by a syncretism that is intrinsically dissonant and deformative.

Syncretism in formation is the attempt to force selected life directives from intrinsically different form traditions into an artificial unity, which in fact is nothing more than an arbitrary collection of incompatible elements. Syncretic formation is usually prefocal. It is a source of dissonance in many people who live in a pluralistic society.

FORM TRADITIONS OF THE FORMATION COUNSELOR

Formation counselors are rooted in subcultures of their own, influenced implicitly by one or various traditions. These subcultures and their underlying traditions may differ from those of their counselees. They may implicitly impose on their counselees their own subcultural view of formation. An unguarded reaction, a certain look, a smile, a slight impatience or surprise may communicate more than words what they really feel. They may unwittingly suggest that their counselees should develop their formation project on the basis of the subcultural structure that nourishes the counselor's own directives and dispositions. If counselees attempt to follow this suggestion, they may fail because the counselor's directives of formation may flow from form traditions which the counselees do not share.

The formation project that the counselor personally cultivates will be for such counselees an abstract ideal, not enfleshed in their own formation history. Such an imposition of alien form directives may result in a new dissonance between the counselees' formative dispositions. Their formation project may flow from their own tradition as embodied in their culture or subculture. Now they may try to develop an alien project of formation, suggested to them by a tactless counselor. Their formation project will then be directed from two conflicting centers: the directives of their own subculturally embodied traditions, and those of their counselor's subculture. We presuppose, of course, that the counselees have not freely decided to change to another subculture, formation segment, or tradition.

Formation counselors can prevent such dissonance if they remain aware of the implicit impact of their personal directives on their communications. Simultaneously they should try to apprehend and appraise the background of the counselee's life formation. This appraisal should be guided by the distinction made between the infrastructure of the tradition of their counselees, its current cultural embodiment, and the personally consonant or dissonant manner in which counselees try to implement this structure.

STRUCTURE OF THE INTERFORMATIVE RELATIONSHIP

The interformative relationship of counseling differs in structure from other interformative relationships. First, it is different because of its objectives, discussed earlier; and second, it is different because of the dispositions the counselor brings to the relationship.

The sessions are meant to facilitate the expression and appraisal of the formation field of the counselee. The basic disposition is one of genuine acceptance of counselees, regardless of what feature of their field they may disclose to us. Any sign of depreciation awakens formation anxiety. On the other hand, bringing to focal apprehension and appraisal one's full field of formation can also be impeded by a too emphatic involvement of the counselor in one or another sphere of this field. Such emotional focusing on one facet may impede the communication of other facets, which may be as or more significant for full apprehension and appraisal. The counselor prompts counselees, by this accepting disposition, to lift into the light of shared focal attention vague and confused apprehensions, appraisals, affirmations, memories, imaginations, anticipations, and accompanying feelings, all of which play a role in their current project of formation.

The formation counselor should be affectively present to the extent necessary to keep the counselees motivated in the exploration of their field and project. Yet this affective presence should be modulated by the necessary strategic distance. Distance in the midst of affective presence makes the interformative relationship of counseling different from other affective relationships interformative in their own fashion. Strategic distance facilitates the relaxed acceptance of all facets of the field and project of the counselees without reacting to them emotionally in a favorable or unfavorable fashion. Either reaction may evoke an appreciative or depreciative fixation on some particular facet of field or project at the expense of the disclosure of other significant aspects. The counselor must be an interformative participant in the field and project of the counselee, while being at the same time its respectful appraiser.

The description of the ideal relationship elicits the question of dispositions that may facilitate this kind of encounter between counselor and counselee. It may be helpful to end this paper with a consideration of two main dispositions a formation counselor should develop in the service of this relationship: one is the formative, the other is the interformative.

FORMATIVE DISPOSITION

The center of our presence is not our own form of life or our own formation. It is the emergent life form of our counselee, its congenial, compatible, and compassionate unfolding within its own formation field.

Counseling becomes formative when we refuse to consider our counselees as mere compilations of symptoms, problems, diagnostic indicators, constellations of personality theories, or exponents of philosophical or theological propositions. This kind of information should remain available in the background of our competent attention. It should not dominate our relationship exclusively.

We must continually transcend such functional evaluations, no matter how significant they are in their own right. We should be disposed to hear primarily the distinctively human appeal of counselees to be wholly with and for them as struggling forms of life called forth uniquely by a transcendent mystery. The care of formation counseling may be summarized by saying that its motivation is the consonant self-formation of the counselees in the free core of their life formation by our participation in that core.

It would be impossible to appraise fully a unique formation story by means of the methods of the exact sciences alone. Such approaches accept as significant only what is reducible to measurement. The unique formation call of a person cannot be disclosed in this way. Only a loving respectful presence to each life form in its gifted uniqueness can disclose this call insofar as it is knowable at this moment.

Every meaningful description presupposes our loving apprehension, appreciation, and confirmation of the present limited disclosure of the counselee's calling. The disposition of loving respect fosters our shared reflection on this disclosure and on the inner and outer obstacles to and facilitating conditions for fidelity to this inner light.

A positivistic approach reduces ongoing life formation to a summary of functional and vital qualities, to a list of symptoms, to an inventory of significant incidents, to a static profile of character, temperament, or personality type. It may freeze an unfolding human form in a filled-out questionnaire, a test, protocol, or case history.

The life form as mystery and call is beyond categorization. Yet formation counseling should take into account the information provided by these positive approaches. In their light, counselors realize the background and the environmental conditions of their counselees, the inner and outer scenery of their struggle, so to speak. They become aware of their symptoms and problematic self-expressions. However, they do not merely identify such conditions and symptoms. They reach out to their deepest roots in the preformative and intraformative regions of the life form of their counselees.

The formation approach enables them to apprehend holistically both the symptoms of deformation and the repudiated or refused facets of the life call of the counselees as disclosed at this moment of their formation history. They interrelate this disclosure of the call and the symptoms of dissonance as mutually illuminating aspects of the same formation story. The counselee is not reduced to a series of functional categories or test scores. Formative concern keeps the counselor present to what is more than symptoms, personality profiles, and problems of adjustment without denying the relative significance of such facets. No diagnostic category by itself alone can do justice to the emergent disclosure of the unique call of a human life form in its personal formation field.

INTERFORMATIVE DISPOSITION

Formative counseling can give new form to the life of the counselee. To understand what this means in the context of the science of formation, we must realize that counseling is not only interformative but that every human meeting shares in some way in that quality.

The manner in which we give form to the life of others is, first of all, influenced by the kind of meeting in which we engage. Take a simple situation. Two men meet each other in a bar. The first phase of this meeting may be one of casual informality. One man makes a pleasant remark to the other; the other responds in kind. Further talk ensues, and for each expression of interest and companionship, there is evoked a counterexpression of interest in the other. As a result of these increasingly pleasant exchanges, the two feel at ease with each other. Then, one man says something about a current political controversy which has lots of people stirred up. He says it in a way that leaves no doubt which side he is on. The other holds the opposite opinion. He feels threatened, offended, hurt. He answers this challenge hotly with an equally forceful argument of his own. His voice is a shade louder than that of his challenger. The other responds in kind. Before either of them realizes it, the friendly meeting has become a heated debate. Soon it turns into a shouting match.

Let us look more closely at the interformative development of this encounter. Notice how the disposition and expression of each person gave form at every moment to the disposition and expression of the other. The two started out as superficial acquaintances. This mode of peripheral interformation was succeeded by one of companionship between mutually interested people. They interformed one another in this mode of presence by friendly dispositions and expressions. Then they switched to giving form mutually to an encounter of heated discussants. Finally, they interformed each other as boisterous fighters.

The point is that they interformed their mutual presence "through" or "by" each other. They really formed each other, first as casual acquaintances, then as sympathetic friends, next as irate debaters, and finally as shouting opponents.

We are so used to modulating the form of each other's life that we are rarely focally aware that one can give form to another's life and its manifestations in a specific fashion and that the other gives form to our life similarly. We cannot think realistically about any form which our life assumed that would be merely the effect of our own form donation alone. We can apprehend ourselves only as born from others, as nourished and formed by others, as speaking the language others formed before us, as wearing clothes designed and produced by others, and as cultivating dispositions generated and unfolded by many others preceding us in the history of human formation.

Take, for example, small infants born black. They only assume inwardly the form of an unjustly treated minority at the moment they are treated differently from children who are not black. This treatment forms their life in a different way. It makes them feel, think, and act in a different fashion. It changes their life form. Note well, it was the interformative encounter which effected this change.

PRINCIPLE OF INTERFORMATION APPLIED TO COUNSELING

We can apply this principle of the science of formation to the counseling situation. The interformative disposition we bring to counseling forms the counselees and ourselves in a way no other encounter (except the love encounter) can give form to our lives.

Interforming encounters, which are not encounters of love or of respectful counseling, imply prefocal classifications. These unspoken categories subtly influence the way in which we give form to others and in which others receive the form we impose upon them.

Say we take a psychological test. When psychologists communicate to us the outcome of the test, such as an IQ or a profile of aptitudes, they give form to us in a certain mode, namely, as persons who are from now on more conscious of the limitations of their "intelligence" or of a range of "skills." Similar communications by medical doctors, teachers, and moralists do indeed indicate a certain number of valid facts about our life. They certainly make us aware of these realities. Doing so, they modulate somewhat the form of our life and of our self-appraisal in relation to concrete data we cannot deny or ignore. For example, our life form has been significantly modulated when we leave the office of the physician who tells us that we have cancer, high blood pressure, diabetes, or an ulcer. We are certainly different than we were before we learned about these physical facts. Our response to this communication in some way affected interformatively our physician too, if we had a real encounter. The doctor may feel compassion and concern, and may experience anew the effect of being medically competent.

In formation counseling, the interformative relationship gains a far deeper dimension. This disposition as cultivated by counselors makes them rise beyond mere facts. They apprehended the counselees primarily as called to relatively free life formation, as people endowed with hidden form potencies and a unique life call. This endowment challenges them to give form to their life in a way not determined exclusively by deformative symptoms, problems, and deficits. Formation counseling interforms the counselees in this relative freedom of formation. It makes them appraise their factual determinants no longer as mere hindrances to human growth. They begin to appreciate them as opportunities for formation of their life in some admittedly limited yet meaningful direction. This creation of new meaning allows them to use limiting formation events inventively to create new modulations of their existence in consonance with the present disclosure of their life call. They become increasingly able to turn obstacles into opportunities. Briefly, when formation counseling is effective, the counselees become ready to affirm themselves as sources of initiative in the midst of seemingly invincible determinants and failures.

INTERFORMATION AS PARTICIPATION IN THE CORE FORM

Interformation means that we participate in the core form of the life of our counselees. By our cordial presence, we foster the free unfolding of this core which is hampered by irrational inhibitions, fears, stereotypes, compulsions, vital pulsions, and popular pulsations. Thanks to interformation, counselees no longer feel like lonely, threatened individuals overwhelmed by the responsibility to devise their formation projects in isolation. Because we are wholeheartedly with them, they dare to open up to their form potencies. We present them, as it were, to themselves. We enable their own fundamental life form to emerge, to take hold of their potencies and limitations. Anxiety-evoking events lose their aura of insurmountability. Our counselees begin to emerge as the flexible masters of their field of form reception and donation.

The interformative disposition of the counselor, if shared by the counselee, generates a "we" experience, a companionship which is different from the "we's" of daily situations. This interformative "we" marks the art and discipline of formation counseling. Before this healing encounter, our counselees may have experienced their field of formation as frightening or desolate. They may have felt choked and oppressed, smothered by formation anxiety.

In interformation we become a new appearance in the field of the counselee. Our sustaining presence is a source of inner freedom. They will be touched sooner or later by the absence of any forcing, imposing, or overpowering on our part. In us their now expanded field of formation shows to them a confirming face. Finally, they may begin to believe in the possibility that not all people, events, and things are as untrustworthy as they tend to anticipate. Our interformative disposition helps to make their field become a home for them.

Before our confirmation of their uniqueness, they may have succumbed to an anxious conformity to the wishes of others. The compulsion to be indiscriminate people pleasers made them lose the relative freedom needed for distinctively human formation. They may have become parrots of popular pulsations, inviting control and enslavement by their surroundings. The repudiation of their fundamental life form may have generated an impotent rage against real or imagined oppressors. Their flow of formation energy may have been halted or fixated.

In interformation we restore and foster respectfully this oppressed life form of the person. We try to break the vicious circle of deformative self-apprehension, appraisal, and affirmation, to release their encapsulated energy into a free formation flow.

Interformation makes us vulnerable. We are exposed by our generosity. Initially, it may lead to the eruption of stored-up resentment, hostility, and aggression. These emotions are directed toward formation counselors as the only persons in one's present formation field against whom one can dare to live out these angry feelings. The interformative mode of presence implies that we maintain our manifestation of loving respect for the unique formation call others are as human persons, even though this call may first reveal itself in a negative fashion.

FREE PARTICIPATION
OF THE COUNSELEE IN INTERFORMATION

Interformation in counseling can only be effective when counselees accept freely their counselors' loving concern and gradually come to share in it by focusing with them on their problems. Otherwise it would not really be interformation. The "yes" of the counselees must ratify the concern of the counselor to make true interformation possible. Formation counselors desire the freedom and transcendence of their counselees. Hence, they can only hope that counselees will enter into interformation by freely collaborating with the loving care extended to them.

Formation counseling amounts to wanting, above all, this formation freedom of the counselees. When the counselees do simply what they are told because of the fact that to them the counselor is an expert or "sees through them" or is "such a nice fellow," the subtle process of growth to freedom is stillborn.

Interformation is fertile only when the person who has to grow chooses to grow. Interformation in depth is an interchange between two human forms of life in which both are actively involved in form reception and donation. Without this free participation by the counselees, interformative counseling cannot occur. This "yes" of the counselees to a freely interforming relationship is their gift to the counselor.

Confrontation
and the Religious Beliefs
of a Client

Samuel M. Natale

"Spiritual belief transcends and informs a person's work. Some people admit they are influenced by it; others swear by its irrelevance."

E. Mark Stern
The Other Side of the Couch

There are few problems more demanding in psychotherapy than dealing with a client's religious beliefs. This is so for a number of reasons, which include not only a lack of sensitivity and understanding on the part of the therapist but also a hesitation, avoidance, and even downright fear on the part of the therapist to explore distinctly religious values with a client. What has resulted all too often is a "different strokes for different folks" attitude. In the long run, such a relativist vacuum cheats the client of an essential opportunity for growth. If therapy has one goal, it must be to implement values and beliefs into action.

The problem is substantially complicated by clients who collude with the therapist's timerity by declaring their personal religious belief system "off limits" to exploration and confrontation. What emerges from all of this is a problematic standoff. Neither counselor nor client will broach the thorny topic. Both continue in the therapeutic process avoiding any careful exploration of religious conviction. The counseling session becomes yet another place where commitment and religious convictions are ignored and left for the church, synagogue, or ashram.

Thus far, those trained in clinical practice have assumed that professional expertise superseded the therapist's personal religious convictions. A recent study (Shafranske & Gorsuch, 1983) conducted by the California State Psychological Association Task Force on Spirituality and

Dr. Samuel M. Natale is Director of the Institute for Business and Professional Ethics at the University of Bridgeport, Connecticut. Currently he is visiting Fellow, St. Edmund's House at the University of Cambridge, England, and research Fellow of the Warborough Trust, Oxford, where he continues his research into moral/ethical development. He is a graduate of the University of Oxford and the author of four books and numerous articles in professional journals.

Psychotherapy indicates quite clearly that the distinction between subjectivity and clinical practice may indeed be compromised whenever religious issues arise in psychotherapy.

Religious questions are fundamentally questions of *meaning of* one's life and *in* one's life. There is a growing concern and belief that when religious issues are involved, therapists tend to relinquish their "dispassionate evaluation of the system's logical coherence and consistency . . ." What has replaced it? (Stolorow & Atwood, 1979).

What seems to have replaced it is avoidance and withdrawal or, more subtly, tolerance of all but the most bizarre cultic rituals and explanations. It seems that clients must virtually stand on their head to get the therapist to even inquire about their religious convictions, much less examine them! Questions regarding the consistency, credibility, coherence, and internal consistency—let alone motivating power—of religious convictions are gingerly passed over.

Religious experience and belief gather meaning by accepting some aspects of experience as constant and credible and by ignoring other aspects as irrelevant. These criteria, in fact, define all reality sense and are the stuff of which human growth and therapeutic development is made. We are talking here of more than tolerating diverse opinions (though that is also a requirement). We are insisting that from the beginning of the therapeutic encounter and as it unfolds both the therapist and the client must "come clean" about just what is admissible as constant and credible in their special relationship. For it is only in defining the limits of constancy and credibility within the interpersonal encounter that any mutual judgments of usefulness or negativity can be made. In short, by sharing a common ground of reality, the therapist strives to recognize judgments that are correct in some instances and incorrect in others.

While the therapist must respect diverse experiences, he or she must also aid clients in understanding and *explaining* their sense of reality. Explanation has two principal functions. The first function is that appropriate explanations compromise the scope of absolute value judgments by limiting and circumscribing the conditions under which such judgments are made. The second function performed by explanations is to augment the reality sense of one set of events *by establishing its relation to other sets of events.* Explanation is a vital step in the transition from what is *accepted* as true to what can be *substantiated* as true. We are arguing that if an event and/or an experience are accepted and experienced as vital, compelling, or formative in an individual's experience (as many individuals insist their religious convictions are), then in some way it is incumbent upon the therapist and client to jointly explore the meaning and significance of these beliefs in terms that provide explanations at least to the client's awareness of the consistency of these beliefs as well as to help individuals answer the questions of the meaning of their personal lives and their place in the universe. Accordingly, it is a condition *sine qua non* that the therapist confront those aspects of religious belief that appear inconsistent with personality integration and personal goal achievement as defined and developed by the client within the therapeutic situation.

How, though, does the therapist determine within the context of the therapeutic relationship which aspects of religious belief are integrating and which are purely defensive and destructive? It seems an impossible task to validate another's religious beliefs and experiences—and it may be. However, this does not stop us from calling on our common traditions to see what might be used as at least an *interim* yardstick. Where do we start?

In a study (Natale, 1984) recently completed with individuals working in industry, I was able to describe four major types of religious world views which appear to correlate with the four major religious traditions. In each of these cases, the study indicated that individuals identify religious belief and experience as identical to the concept of maturity. It seems that individuals tend to identify religious commitment/belief with success and maturity. It is intriguing to note that the four modes which individuals repeatedly returned to in describing their most basic religious experiences were identical in substance to the notions of integration and maturity in the four great religious traditions.

The first group discussed and described religious integration and successful achievement of religious goals as similar to relationship. "It means you care about people . . . and you act to help them." These individuals perceived a fundamental connection between relationship and doing justice. This idea is of course similar to the notion of maturity in the Hebrew scripture which has its close link between love of God and political/social activity toward bettering the situation of the unprotected.

A second group associated success and religious integration with responsibility and stability which they defined as community involvement. Their religious and philosophical base was that "religious integration and success are achieved in a group," and this notion is clearly similar to Christianity's emphasis on reflection, action, and communitarian solidarity (Bousma, 1978).

A third group of individuals interpreted religious conviction as success as the result of hard work, responsibility, obedience to the law, and especially personal contracts. "One is not impulsive, works hard, and is able to keep one's word." This is close to the essentially legalistic formulation of maturity in Islam. As in Islam, a balance must be struck between confidence and humility (Lapidus, 1978).

The last general group saw religious experience as an "unending process of growth toward an ultimate." This response, interestingly, was limited to the oldest members of the group and was characterized by seeking a balance, learning to live with social norms, and the inevitability of the life cycle. These terms are remarkably reminiscent of the Confucian perception of adulthood (Tu Wei-Ming, 1978).

Obviously these foregoing descriptions remain somewhat nebulous and difficult to focus on. However, there is enough in each of these descriptions to designate specific behaviors and actions which allow the therapist to intervene and challenge the discrepancy between what clients say they believe and what, in fact, their behaviors indicate they act on. If one claims a religious motivation generally similar to those described above, then the therapist does have a point at which to intervene and a direction toward which to motivate—at least if consistency is a therapeutic goal. The therapist in this case is not just assuming the passive relativist vacuum but insists that clients assume responsibility for claimed religious motivation as they would in any other area of growth and development. Needless to say, clients will resist this attempt on the part of the therapist to hold them responsible and accountable and it is here that the therapist may intervene using confrontation.

This resistance to being held accountable is the groundwork for therapeutic change and the psychotherapeutic process can be opened up considerably. If, for example, a client claims a deep religious concern with other individuals' welfare as an essential part of his or her sense of transcendance, the therapist can profitably reflect the elements of discrepancy in the client's personal life with some benefit. This allows for continual correction of affect and behaviors as a function of religious conviction. It empowers the client to adapt, expand, add, or delete from the core claimed to be religious experience and revelation.

CONFRONTATION

Confrontation is a frequent treatment technique with clients during some phase of psychotherapy. Most of the reported cases appear to fit into two possible categories of psychotherapeutic interventions. In both these categories, the therapist either actively indicated to the client how his or her behavior affected other people, including the therapist, or the therapist persisted in demonstrating to the patient a feeling or urge that he or she was somewhat reluctant to acknowledge.

What all these examples appear to share in common is some aspect of forcefulness in a therapist's attitude and behavior. The concept of confrontation is relevant because it corresponds to the state of the therapist's mind at the time when he or she decides to confront the patient and in many instances when he or she decides to employ a more enhancing approach.

It was Edward Bibring (1954) who established a systematic and thoughtful way of exploring this psychotherapeutic process. For example,

Bibring established the basic criteria which distinguish clarification from interpretation—two other therapeutic principles. An *interpretation* often leads a patient to resist what has been indicated because it touches upon some raw nerve. He contrasts this with a *clarification* which the client accepts with some pleasure because this new knowledge evokes a sense of mastery instead of danger.

Confrontation consists of a myriad of activities whose polar positions are defined in terms of their routine versus their extraordinary aspects. Confrontation is considered routine in general practice and utilizes the client's attention, reaction, and change. For example, focusing attention is an ordinary activity that goes on in every form of therapy. Essentially, it consists of an attempt to get the individual to focus on some situation, problem, or conflict and bring it within the scope of therapy. As Devereux (1951) argued, "in simplest terms, confrontation is a device whereby the patient's attention is directed to the bare factual content of his actions or statements or to a coincidence which he has perceived, but has not, or professes not to have, registered" (p.19). It seems a small step forward to suggest that a client who professes religious belief and conviction be asked to focus on these convictions and bring them into the therapeutic encounter with all of their affirming and integrating properties, as well as the elements of inappropriate self-denigration, inconsistency, and inappropriateness. Clients who, claiming to operate out of a deep Christian commitment, hold strong racist social and political views must be afforded the opportunity to reconcile these discrepancies between the bare facts of their actions and the claimed spiritual motivations!

Clients may be truly unaware of the discrepancies between their professed belief and experience and their contradictory actions. Greenson (1967) has argued that if the client is unaware, "it is essential to confront the patient with the fact that a resistance is present before we attempt anything further" (p. 104). Hence, for Greenson, appropriate confrontation leads systematically to the clarification, interpretation, and working through of the resistance. As we shall see, it is in the clarifying and interpretating phase of the treatment that the client has the greatest opportunity to achieve a self-transcending capacity.

Routine confrontation is just one pole of the use of confrontation. There is another pole, which can be considered heroic confrontation—that which is perhaps a memorable part of a day. One might consider a heroic confrontation to be an emotionally charged, parametric, manipulative, technical tool demanded by the development of an actual or potential impasse situation which is designed ultimately to remobilize a workable therapeutic alliance. For example, if it is clear that a person's religious beliefs are completely separated from daily life, and the client refuses to apply what he or she has already voluntarily indicated as "essential," it may be necessary for the therapist to confront these discrepancies and insist that the client either arrange some sort of "correction" between values, attitudes, needs, and expectations and consistency with the religious beliefs or to concede them as not fully operative. The aim of this confrontation, like all other confrontations, is *always* directed toward strengthening the therapeutic alliance. As in many cases, it is the client and the client's behaviors that will determine whether the confrontation will be merely routine or dramatic.

The real key to understanding the nature of confrontation and that pole it leans toward appears to be at the level of the development of the real or working alliance. When that is good, most elements will at least be admitted for discussion, whether they are symptoms, discrepancies, acting out, or resistance. What is most important in the dramatic/heroic confrontation is that it says clearly that either the client must do something, that is, change in some way to bring about integration/consistency, or the therapeutic relationship will have to stop since it has become nonproductive. Obviously this step is taken with great reflection and care on the part of the therapist and it is *always* geared to preserving the relationship. If timed and carried out correctly, the frequent result is that the client will accept—at least for the moment—the necessity to make changes in behaviors or minimally to examine the areas of discrepancy. We will insist that the client conform to personal convictions within a broad scope that acknowledges the general insights of clinical, general, developmental, and transpersonal psychology.

Overall, confrontation is the first in an orderly sequence of steps followed by clarification, interpretation, and working through. Its purpose is to show the client that he or she is living in a state of discrepancy which produces debilitating constrictions on their life. In this confrontation with the client, the therapist is of central importance and assumes a dominant role. By choosing one element of the client's life and not another, the counselor controls the situation. Obviously, in choosing one aspect of discrepancy to focus on, other elements are passed over. Hence, the critical ability of the therapist to be comfortable with the religious dimension of personality and/or experience *or* to refer the client to an individual who is. The rule of thumb seems intuitively obvious: If clients experience religious experience as controlling and motivating in their lives and wish to explore their lives, then the therapist must be prepared and equipped to do this. This often requires a harrowing reevaluation of the therapist's own self-transcending concerns.

In any initial therapeutic relationship, one might consider that each client more or less exhibits ambivalent actions and feelings: There is a real dread of the self-revelation and exploration which lie ahead in psychotherapy and there is, simultaneously, a deep longing to develop closeness with the helper. In the religiously committed client, this is most often observed as a desire to talk about the role that religion has played in one's

life while at the same time moving away from any fuller affective exploration of how religious commitments are evaded or ignored in favor of
more immediately self-satisfying pursuits. Why would therapists worth
their salt not comment on this kind of discrepancy when, in any other
analogous situation, they would certainly address the issue with some
gusto?

The technique of confrontation requires an orderly development and,
as in any other technique, needs to be applied in sequence for the fullest
effect. Confrontation with the past is the first stage which the therapist
finds himself or herself addressing. This requires that the therapist be empathic and place himself or herself within the client's world and to structure that world in the same way as the client does. This imaginitive trans-
position of the world by the therapist will make it possible to penetrate the
client's denials and other resistances. Most commonly, a client will present personal history in a most unhappy light and, at the same time, recount the satisfactions of the religious beliefs which explain the necessity
of such chronic discomfort (e.g., "everyone has a cross to carry"). The
therapist's task here seems initially clear: to raise the central question
about the client's past in terms of religious beliefs. For example, a discor-
dant note can be sounded by asking the client to imagine whether religion
as they see it is necessarily tied into depression and unhappiness. Where
did they learn this and WHY would anyone continue to hold on to such a
consistently unsatisfying position? Although many therapists avoid the
religious dimension and refuse to explore this issue, it is clear that with
some clients whose past has been so painful, it would be impossible to
indicate an understanding of their pasts without participating in correcting
their present. To simply allow clients to stand by and discuss past difficulties while permitting them to continue in the present is to convince
them that you, as therapist, have no real grasp of either their world or
their past!

Confrontation is clearly a multifaceted event. It cannot be discussed as
though it refers to one type of approach or intervention. What all confrontation does have in common is that it is both intense and forceful. One
would also distinguish that a confrontation would tend to be either empathic or angry. The counselor may clearly dislike and disapprove of a
client's behavior (e.g., bigotry). The second, and more important, element is that the therapist feels a prudential need to change the client's behavior. The anger that these evaluations produce in the therapist provide
the forcefulness required for the confrontation. It insists that clients take
full responsibility for their behaviors and challenges them to consider that
there may be more humanly productive ways to proceed than the one they
are currently using. Within this angry transaction between helper and
helpee something important happens as both work through the issues
under debate. In fact, the client is forced to see something which he or she

might otherwise have ignored, namely, that this pattern of action on the part of the client most probably produced the same results on other people and that the client remains responsible for this behavior.

Even the more esoteric forms of religious belief such as restrictive diets, miracles, and so forth are available for therapeutic exploration. The operative principle here seems to be that all claimed religious experiences must have an integrating quality about them. In short, religious experiences and beliefs which result in the deterioration of the client or which absolve clients from fundamental responsibility for their convictions (e.g., "The bible tells me so.") must be challenged as fully as any other such projective defense. For indeed the scripture may tell someone so, but the person who implements beliefs remains responsible for them before the community, as well as before God!

A less dramatic form of intervention is the empathic confrontation in which the therapist is able to challenge the clients in a caring way by feeling free from a need to change them. Instead of feeling under pressure to make clients different, the therapist accepts patients for what they are and is then in a position to take up whatever behavior may interfere with their capacities to form close relationships with the therapist or others. In this process the therapist and client encounter one another in the here and now. It encourages new and immediate ways of being with the counselor that truly facilitate change. With the religious client, this here-and-now emphasis is critically important since the therapist enters empathically into the client's world and experiences with the client the vitality of his or her transcending beliefs. What the therapist confronts however is how these experiences ring differently/similarly for the therapist. The therapist has, accordingly, affirmed the richness of self-transcending experience and yet, at the same time, has indicated that within the context of a special and safe relationship, there is at least one other way to react to the particular religious principle. This approach has proven most effective in treating discrepancies between religious conviction and social responsibility, discrimination, and moral/spiritual imperialism.

What we have been saying is closely linked to reality therapy as well as other forms of diverse therapy. We base our approach on the premise that there is a single psychological need which is preeminent throughout the life cycle: a need for identity that encompasses a need to feel a sense of distinctiveness. We are at once in the crowd and of the crowd. Religious experience calls us to become deeply aware of the reality that we are indeed each unique in creation and yet remain accountable to our communities. To deny the "otherness" of individuals is to plunge oneself into narcissism—a position inconsistent with religious and self-transcending experience.

We are arguing that religious experience must be admitted to the therapeutic exploration and we openly reject any model which assumes that religious belief is pathological. We insist that religious experience be admitted with the same critical eye that any other vital aspect of living is. We want in our exploration to stress becoming aware of our present behavior and how it got that way. The past becomes prelude to the present but we live in the present. We poise ourselves at the center point between memory and expectation: memory of things past and expectation (hope) of what might be. Confrontation is employed whenever the client tilts too radically either to the past and ancient authorities or to a futurist approach which denies any vitality in the here and now.

In our therapeutic work, we peruse clients' values, attitudes, needs, and expectations as they affect themselves, us, and the broader community. We aid clients in judging their own values and the quality of their own behavior in order to determine how their life fits into the questions *they* have raised: Where do I fit? Where am I going? How do I know when I got there? How does my experience of the self-transcending illumine this for me?

Finally, we prefer confrontation as a mode of intervention because all maturity and any fundamental religious system must have as its base a sense of responsibility. In confronting, the therapist is simply insisting that clients assume responsibility for what they say motivates them.

Obviously the battle over the viability and reality of religious experience will continue uninterrupted. However, the therapist must still act in a consistent way and, increasingly, that is including dealing with client's self-transcending value systems most notably formulated in the great religious experiences. Although we are not able to delimit the sphere of individual religious experience, it does seem essential that we can make at least some fundamental conditions which include at least that the client's religious beliefs are accounted for and respected, and that the client be able to internalize these beliefs or modify/abandon them for experiences which are more fully integrating. For integration must surely remain the condition of possibility for genuine religious experience and belief lived responsibly, fully, and with satisfaction.

REFERENCES

Bibring, E. (1954). Psychoanalysis and the dynamic psychotherapies. *Journal of the American Psychoanalytic Association, 2,* 745-770.

Bousma, W. (1978). Christian adulthood. In E. Erikson (Ed.), *Adulthood.* New York: Norton.

Devereux, G. (1951). Some criteria for the timing of confrontations and interpretations. *International Journal of Psychoanalysis, 32,* 19-24.

Greenson, R. (1967). *The technique and practice of psychoanalysis.* New York: International Universities Press.

Lapidus, I. (1978). Adulthood in Islam: Religious maturity in the Islamic tradition. In E. Erikson (Ed.), *Adulthood.* New York: Norton.

Natale, S. (in press). Pastoral counseling and psychotherapy in industry: Differing results? *Journal of Pastoral Counseling.*

Shafranske, E. & Gorsuch, R. (1983). *Factors associated with the perception of spirituality in psychotherapy.* Paper presented at the annual convention of the American Psychological Association, Anaheim, CA.

Stern, E.M. (Ed.). (1981). *The other side of the couch.* New York: Pilgrim Press.

Stolorow, R. & Atwood, G. (1979). *Faces in a cloud: Subjectivity in personality theory.* New York: Jason Aronson.

Tu Wei-Ming. (1978). The Confucian perception of adulthood. In E. Erikson (Ed.), *Adulthood.* New York: Norton.

Metaphor and Therapy: Theory, Technique, and Practice of the Use of Religious Imagery in Therapy

Raymond J. Stovich

In therapy, an athlete speaking the language of athletics, or a business-person speaking the language of business, would not create much of a problem for most therapists. However, if a person whose primary mode of self-understanding or self-expression is religious imagery came to therapy, the exact opposite would probably be true. The mix of religion and psychology creates a powerful dynamic for client and therapist alike. Yet, if we are to be able to enter our client's world therapeutically, we must be able to deal with this religiously oriented imagery. This paper seeks to provide a theoretical orientation which does justice to both religious language and sound psychological practice, one which enables the therapist to meet the client on his or her ground. It also seeks to present techniques to bring this theoretical understanding into the consultation room. Most of the case material will be drawn from a Christian tradition, though the theory and techniques are applicable to other religious traditions as well. Let us begin.

THEORY: THE NATURE OF RELIGIOUS LANGUAGE

The nature and function of religious language differ from that of ordinary usage, which seeks to communicate some known information to another clearly defined being. Religious language, however, involves the Divine, a realm of being which, by definition, is "wholly other" than our human realm and whose object transcends human categories (Otto,

Raymond J. Stovich received MDiv and STL degrees from St. Mary of the Lake, Mundelein, Illinois, and a doctorate in psychology from the California Institute of Transpersonal Psychology, Menlo Park, California. He has 10 years of professional experience and is co-author (with Tom Moore) of the forthcoming book, *Archetypal Gerontology*. Dr. Stovich has a private practice in Menlo Park. Material for this article is taken from a work in progress on various aspects of metaphor and therapy.

117

1958). As Alan Watts frequently said, it is an attempt to "ef" the "ineffable." Religious language is a symbolic language which functions through metaphors that are found most frequently as specific images. For example, in the Gospel according to Matthew it is said that Jesus likened the Kingdom of Heaven to a farmer who, upon finding a hidden treasure buried in a field, sold all he had to buy that field and get the treasure (Matthew 13:44). Does this mean that only farmers will enter the Kingdom of Heaven? Must one excavate a hidden treasure box in order to be saved? The error in this line of thinking is to treat the subject matter in a literal mode of understanding, that is, to see this story as pertaining to farmers who till real fields and literal treasure boxes buried in these fields. So, how are we to understand religious language? What does it mean that religious language is metaphorical?

Metaphor derives from the Greek words *meta,* a prefix which implies a passing over, a going from one place to another, and *phorein,* which means to move or carry. A metaphor, then, carries us from one place to another, moves us across boundaries. Religious language seeks to create some inner movement and to help us across boundaries. These boundaries may be those of the sacred/secular or divine/human, or they may be the boundaries of our own inner structures, oftentimes become rigid and inflexible. Religious language seeks to create this inner movement by its nature as metaphor, and it does this by means of two principal functions: its *symbolic* function and its *tropic* function. Let us pursue these functions.

Carl Jung (1965) spoke of a symbol as the best possible formulation of something which is unknown. Symbol must be clearly differentiated from sign. A *sign* is a representation of a known entity which serves to communicate some information about it. A sign most often operates on a literal level. For instance, a stop sign clearly stands for a known literal entity (activity) and communicates that we are able to perform that act. If we understand the aforementioned parable of Jesus as telling us that we need to buy plows and get to work, we are interpreting it on the level of sign. A *symbol* is the best possible formulation of something unknown or unconscious. What makes it the best possible formulation is that it contains some of the reality of that unknown. For example, we really don't know what our full being is, but we express that mystery with the image of "wholeness." Wholeness moves our psyche toward its totality. It gets us thinking about it; it sparks our imagination and desires; it gets us moving in that direction. In a dream, wholeness may be further symbolized by a perfectly formed crystal or a sphere. In either case the image which is the symbol conveys some special and specific aspect of that which it symbolizes and moves us in that direction. In the parable of the farmer and the treasure, the treasure is a symbol. In our human dimension of existence we cannot fully know the nature of the Kingdom of Heaven. The image of a treasure symbolizes that, however, and gets us imagining Heaven (itself an image) as something of great worth, something which will dawn upon us with a great surprise, something which must be sacrificed for, and so forth. Metaphor moves our consciousness across boundaries to spark new insights and to open us to multiple dimensions of our reality.

The second way in which metaphor operates is by its *tropic* function (Crossan, 1973, 1980). Tropic refers to a certain literary technique known as a trope. Troping an image is like cracking a nut to expose its meat. A trope functions to break open our conceptual or perceptual fixes so that we can see naked reality more clearly. It's like an "aha" experience in which we see something very common as if seeing it for the very first time. In terms of our example parable, we can imagine Jesus preaching to a group of farmers, telling them his little story and watching their reactions, "Oh, I get it now."

In addition, metaphor, by its nature, is ambivalent, or more precisely *multideterminant* (Winquist, 1978). In other words, one of the keys to understanding how metaphor works is to realize that when one interpretation is settled upon, or perhaps when "the" interpretation is arrived at, then the image is robbed of its metaphorical nature, and reverts to being a sign. It is only when the image can move our psyches and imaginations in multiple directions, toward multiple insights and viewpoints, that its true nature as metaphor is evidenced. What, then, is the "treasure" of which Jesus spoke? On one day it may be family life, on another it may be some special talent, at a third time it may be a sense of destiny, and then again it may be a mystical state, and on and on. Each time the symbol moves us further into the multidimensionality of the unknown, breaking through concepts and structures with fresh insight.

Thus religious language is metaphorical, symbolic, and tropic. It serves to move consciousness and to assist the hearer into more clear perceptions of the multiple dimensions and facets of reality. There is one more function of religious language which we must note. Religious language most frequently works through story. These stories are of a personal and a collective nature. The essential religious symbols and stories, though felt personally, are shared by many people. Even the most personal of visions frequently contains collective images or elements. As an individual identifies with elements of the story, the story in turn relates that person to the collective. In this manner these stories situate a person within a context of meaning. This is the *mythic* function of religious language.

In this context myth is not an untrue fiction, but rather it is a symbolic story which seeks to present a transpersonal truth. Myths are *atemporal*, that is they are not stories about the past or future but about what is happening right now in a different dimension of reality (Eliade, 1963). For example, the Book of Genesis starts with "In beginning . . ." (the article is omitted in the original Hebrew text). It is not so much the story of what happened in the beginning of time as it is an account of what is happening right now when (theologically) the community is constantly being re-created or (psychologically) something is coming to birth in the psyche, and so forth. Myth is not so much a story for the sake of information, but a story which provides us with perspective, or multiple perspectives, from which we can envision and understand what's happening in our lives on its myriad levels and dimensions (Moore, 1983). This insight is one of the major keys to using religious images in therapeutic context.

In summary, then, the purpose and function of religious language is far different from simple communication of fact. Religious language, when properly functioning, serves to move the psyche, drawing it out of its narrow ego confines toward a larger, transpersonal realm, a realm which exists as another dimension of our lives. In this process religious language serves to facilitate movement across inner boundaries and stuck places within the psyche. Pathology exists when these images become concretized into literal reality, whether that be defensive projection, neurosis, or psychotic delusion. For clients for whom religious language is a predominant or prominent mode of relating to the world, inner or outer, the mythic nature of these stories and images can serve (if a religious image or two be permitted) to resurrect psychic movement and begin the path to healing and wholeness.

TECHNIQUES: WORKING WITH IMAGES

In this section we shall examine some specific interventions, that is, techniques for working with images in general and specifically with religious images. These techniques are intended to be used within a context of ongoing therapy in accord with the clinical training, comfort, and judgment of the therapist. A diagnostic workup is presupposed. Four categories of interventions will be listed and briefly discussed.

Encountering the Image

This category includes a wide variety of techniques useful in assisting the client into a here and now confrontation with images either suggested by the therapist or arising spontaneously within the client. Underlying these techniques is the understanding that religious images are mythic, that is, atemporal stories which help us envision a client's life from multiple perspectives and in multiple dimensions. The image is the best possible expression of these perspectives and dimensions and is in fact, the door to them. Religious teachers have been using similar techniques for centuries, for example, the spiritual exercises of Ignatius of Loyola. A myriad of techniques fit here from progressive relaxation coupled with visualization, through gestalt work, Jung's active imagination, to a whole range of techniques found in art therapy. A frequently useful technique to help a client consolidate the results of an encounter with an image is to have the client write a poem as a response to his or her experience. This technique helps bring together right- and left-hemisphere activity, rounding out the learning process.

Amplifying the Image

In amplification, the therapist uses analogies to make the situation of the client appear more clearly, to amplify it or make it louder. The key to amplification is to find another image which bears an *essential similarity* to the situation of the client (Berry, 1982). If skillfully applied this technique can free the client from being locked into a very narrow literal and personal view of his or her problems and see them as a little more universal, more human.

Multidimensionality, or "Yes . . . and . . ."

Perhaps the greatest trap to fall into when working with clients who use a lot of religious language is to begin to argue with the oftentimes rigid, absolute judgmentalism these clients exhibit. This is especially true of clients with a fundamentalist background or who are dealing with obsession, compulsion, and guilt. However, a useful therapeutic goal is to assist the client into a position wherein two or more types of religious images are coexisting. At times this can break through the rigid holding pattern and pave the way for more movement.

Discernment

One final technique, the art of discernment, needs attention. Over the years the Christian traditions have developed guidelines for determining whether a vision or personal revelation comes from the sources of God (i.e., are positive, health enhancing) or from the Devil (i.e., are pathological). The visions themselves cannot be judged, but their effects can be studied and from these effects an accurate determination could be made. Morton Kelsey (1978) has written a thorough psychological study on this topic entitled *Discernment* upon which this work draws. A good solid diagnosis cannot be ruled out, but these principles can help the practitioner in dealing with religious images. Religious imagery may be said to be positive and health enhancing when it results in an increase of openness, creativity, growth, humility, and consciousness. If these qualities are not present and if there is a tendency to manipulate people, to hold to a personal and secret knowledge, and to wield power over others as a result of the vision, pathology is highly suspected. Though the art of discernment is subtle and refined, these guidelines may help the therapist to be secure in working with positive religious imagery.

REFERENCES

Berry, P. (1982). *Echo's subtle body*. Dallas: Spring.
Crossan, J. (1980). *Cliffs of fall*. New York: Seabury.
Crossan, J. (1973). *In parables*. New York: Harper & Row.
Eliade, M. (1963). *Myth and reality*. New York: Harper & Row.
Jones, A. (Ed.) (1966). *The Jerusalem Bible*. Garden City, NJ: Doubleday.
Jung, C. (1965). *Memories, dreams, reflections*. New York: Vintage Books.
Kelsey, M. (1978). *Discernment*. New York: Paulist Press.
MacLeish, A. (1978). *J.B.* New York: Samuel French.
Moore, T. (1983). *Rituals of the imagination*. Dallas: The Pegasus Foundation.
Otto, R. (1958). *The idea of the holy*. New York: Oxford U. Press.
Winquist, C. (1978). *Homecoming*. Missoula, MT: Scholar's Press.

The Psychotherapist
and Religious Commitment

William N. Grosch

As a psychiatrist and minister, I am deeply interested in psychotherapy and religious faith. Frequently colleagues have asked how my faith and religious ministry affect my practice of psychotherapy. This article is a result of my personal exploration of the doctor's religious values, and how these values influence patients in the face of therapeutic neutrality.

Both psychiatry and religion claim responsibility for comprehensive formulations about human behavior and values. Even so, psychiatry has tried to evade the issue of values. More recently, however, it has become clear to psychiatrists that values are here to stay. And while members of the profession try to avoid imposing them in the context of their work, it must be realized that their patients are influenced regardless of the intent. "Psychiatry and Human Values" was the theme of the 1980 annual meeting of the American Psychiatric Association, pointing up the timeliness for taking responsibility for research on the impact of the expressed or unexpressed values of the therapist.

Pattison (1969b) noted that most psychotherapists steer clear of dealing with religious issues in psychotherapy, rarely, if ever, employing religious concepts or techniques in treatment. On the other hand, Lowinger and others (1966) have demonstrated that the religious attitudes of psychotherapists significantly affect their treatment.

A recent report (Shafranske & Gorsuch, 1983) of the California State Psychological Association Task Force on Spirituality and Psychotherapy, based on a survey of clinical psychologists in California, indicated that of those questioned, therapeutic interventions were based on personal rather than professional orientations in what they addressed of spiritual issues in the course of psychotherapy.

In a similar study, Wolff (cited in Bühler, 1962) noted that 48% of the psychotherapists and psychoanalysts questioned confirmed that "value

William N. Grosch, MD, MDiv., is associate professor of clinical psychiatry and medical director of the psychiatric outpatient clinic of Albany Medical College, Albany, New York. He is also director of pastoral services at the Capital District Psychiatric Center in Albany. Dr. Grosch is an ordained minister of the United Church of Christ.

concepts of the therapists do have and should have a direct influence upon the therapy'' (pp. 11-12). An additional 24% saw an indirect influence taking place. Another group of psychoanalysts concurred that while changes in moral values may be expected from psychotherapy, since they are involved in patients' conflicts, the therapist communicates his or her values to the patient in many subtle and unintended ways (Szasz, 1962).

Values do change in psychotherapy, not only because patients re-examine their own beliefs, but also because they learn to accept the moral values of their therapists. This, according to a study by Rosenthal (1955), was especially true of those patients who improved as a result of therapy. Those who did not improve or who deteriorated tended to move away from the therapists' value systems. Others have pointed to the practical impossibility of therapeutic neutrality with respect to values (Bergin, 1980; Halleck, 1976; Pattison, 1969).

The assertion that psychotherapy, especially psychoanalysis, is an ethically neutral and value-free endeavor is no longer tenable. In the light of numerous studies, it has been demonstrated that therapy is most successful when therapist and patient share similar values, and, more important, that the therapist does, indeed, transmit values to the patient.

Nevertheless, therapists' attitudes and convictions about religion do pose special problems as well as challenges to the management of psychotherapy since their attitudes and countertransferences are likely to invade discussions of sex, aggression, authority, death, money, *and* religion. A therapist's confusion about ultimate or existential concerns is apt to be communicated and lead to further confusion on the part of patients struggling with the same issues.

Unacknowledged identification with a patient whose religious struggles are reminiscent of the therapist's own experience may cause psychopathology to be underestimated and unaddressed since the therapist may want to avoid relevant religious issues. On the other hand, negative reactions often lead to unnecessary struggles with the patient. In such instances the therapist may pursue discussions which have only a tenuous relevance to the task at hand (Peteet, 1981, p. 562).

To the extent that the therapist's values are clear, they can be left in the background while the patient's material occupies the foreground. Yet there remains the danger of mutual blind spots. This is especially true when a patient picks a pastoral counselor or a Christian psychiatrist because of shared value commitments. This must be balanced against the potential advantages of shared values leaving both doctor and patient free to concentrate on the central emotional-dynamic issues. In such cases the therapist need not worry as much about unwittingly confirming a value structure that he or she does not believe in. Even more important, a patient reasonably certain about the therapist's value system is free to set aside moral issues without fearing that he or she will unwittingly be inducted into a set of values that he or she does not consciously affirm nor subscribe to (Browning, 1976).

* * *

> A 20-year-old college student reluctantly agreed to seek psychiatric help for depression and concurrent hostility. This young man had been attempting to control these feelings through prayer and Bible reading. A previous psychiatrist had told him that much of his difficulty stemmed from his being "too religious." A summary from this psychiatrist revealed that his treatment plan had "focused on the reduction of religious preoccupation." (Peteet, 1981, p. 561)

The relevant question to be posed was whether the psychiatrist deliberately attempted symptom reduction. In this connection, did he really think that "religious preoccupation" was the basic problem? Obviously this young man felt that the psychiatrist viewed his interest in religion as a problem rather than as a possible solution. Was the doctor consciously trying to confront defensiveness and/or resistance? Or was he diagnosing the problem in terms of the most conspicuous behavioral and verbal presentation of the patient, that is, his religious activity?

Obviously it is imperative for psychotherapists to be aware of their religious values (or lack of them) and to have the sensitivity to keep them from interfering with exploration of the patient's attitudes and values. Certainly, if a patient makes an antireligious statement to a therapist, the therapist should respond by trying to help the patient discover his or her own truth. The therapist's own religion ought not determine his or her response. But what about the therapist with a strong religious commitment who accepts without question positive statements about religion or statements of religious orthodoxy? A colleague who describes himself as nonreligious told me that he bends over backwards not to challenge patients' religious statements in order to avoid introducing his own bias. Unfortunately this attitude may ultimately be responsible for his failure to ever respond to the relevant issues within the patient's belief system.

It must be clear by now that most psychotherapists are, in fact, cryptomissionaries. Yet it is not a therapist's business to convert or unconvert patients. Even so, some contend that a therapist may unconsciously be carrying on a missionary activity leading to ineffective and possibly destructive therapeutic results. This, of course, assumes that religious content is like any other. If such issues do come up, one must deal with them on the same technical basis as anything else because some patients may be using religion to avoid talking about other issues or else they may use it as part of an intellectualized defensive system by seducing the therapist into cognitive combat. It is possible that a therapist who is engaged in discussion about value problems or religious questions may be colluding with the patient's defenses. Yet throughout the course of psychotherapy there often occur exchanges between patient and therapist that are not defensive intellectualizations but, in form, rather like segments from a Platonic dialogue. Some are justifiably skittish about getting involved in such interaction because of their own ambiguities about values. Such ambiguities may make them feel unsure about dealing with religious material as anything but derivatives of unconscious issues. Such assumptions infer that whenever moral or religious issues arise in psychotherapy they are by definition never what they appear to be, and that the patient is in fact "really" talking about something else.

On the other hand, there are psychotherapists who not only permit but encourage a detailed consideration of value problems. They prefer to do more than treat the patient's value orientation as a symptom of "something else." Such practitioners see the patient's value orientation as one of the important determiners of ways of viewing happiness or unhappiness. Accordingly, they are often willing to assume a pedagogical role in direct behavioral retraining, viewing cognitive clarification as fundamental to the therapeutic process.

Certainly the crucial question is whether it is desirable to sharpen the attitudes and techniques of therapists to the point that they will not, even subtly, influence the course of their patients' religious thinking and feeling. In matters of religion, as in other concerns, the tactics and strategies of the therapist are bound to reflect a personal vantage point. If, for example, a patient states that he has been saved by God's grace, an atheist therapist would not possibly accept this account. Such a therapist might assume other psychological factors to be at work (Meehl, 1959). Hopefully, however, the theistic therapist would also be able to maintain such a questioning attitude. In any case, it is right for a prospective patient to want to insure his or her integrity by wanting a psychiatrist who would promise in advance that the treatment would not undermine their faith. Yet no honest psychiatrist—believer or otherwise—can make such a promise even if willing to take an active role in promoting religion in the life of the patient. The road to self-discovery is devious and may lead to the unmasking of, and disenchantment with, what one thought was genuine. It might be that the patient needed to discover what little faith he or she really had.

Psychotherapists do have the obligation to assess their patients' material within the context provided by each individual. Nevertheless, striving for moral neutrality is different from moral indifference (Pattison, 1969a). The problem is not that values are transmitted in therapy—that has already been established—but rather how they are transmitted.

REFERENCES

Bergin, A.E. (1980). Psychotherapy and religious values. *Journal of Consulting and Clinical Psychology, 48,* 98.

Browing, D.S. (1976). *The moral context of pastoral care.* Philadelphia: The Westminster Press.

Bühler, C. (1962). *Values in psychotherapy.* New York: The Free Press of Glencoe.

Halleck, S.L. (1976). Discussion of "Socially reinforced obsessing." *Journal of Consulting and Clinical Psychology, 44*(1), 147.

Lowinger, P. et al. (1966). Does the race, religion or social class of a patient affect his treatment? In J. Masserman (Ed.), *Science and psychoanalysis,* (Vol. 9). New York: Grune & Stratton.

Meehl, P.E. (1959). Some technical and axiological problems in the therapeutic handling of religious and valuational material. *The Journal of Counseling Psychology, 6*(4), 258.

Pattison, E.M. (1969a). Morality, guilt, and forgiveness in psychotherapy. *International Psychiatry Clinics, 5*(4), 108.

Pattison, E. M. (1969b). The role of religion in psychotherapy. *International Psychiatry Clinics, 5*(4), 78.

Peteet, J.R. (1981). Issues in the treatment of religious patients. *American Journal of Psychotherapy, 35*(4), 561-562.

Shafranske, E.P. & Gorsuch, R.L. (1983). *Factors associated with the perception of spirituality.* Unpublished paper.

Szasz, T.S. (1962). The problem of privacy in training analysis. *Psychiatry, 25,* 195.

Dealing with Proceptive Countertransference-like Issues: The Factor of Psychotherapeutic Ideology

Orlo Strunk, Jr.

The subtitle of Ehrenwald's (1976) volume on the history of psychotherapy is *From Magic to Encounter*. One wonders if it might not be necessary when extending this history into the late 1990s to modify that subtitle to something like *From Healing Magic to Ideological and Cosmological Modifications*. Certainly there are a growing number of indications that psychotherapy can no longer seriously be claimed to be a neutral process free from approach or from broad assumptional systems. If ever there were times in which psychotherapy was conceived essentially as a technology far removed from metaphysical and moral moorings, those times must be counted as passé and naïve. Even if professional counselors and psychotherapists continue to resist recognizing psychotherapy as at least another moral system, consumers will not. And as psychotherapy becomes more visible in the academic and health fields, the critiques of its philosophical, cosmological, and ideological groundings will be done not only with greater vigor but by a cadre of sophisticated scholars especially equipped with uncovering techniques. This critical project, designed to root out and make manifest psychotherapy's foundations, may be met defensively by the psychotherapeutic community or that community may instead join in that search *from within*.

This brief article is an expression of the conviction that this second alternative is the better way to go. It is as well an illustration of one of the factors standing in need of greater recognition and explication—namely, the presence of psychotherapy ideologies in both therapist and client.

THE NATURE OF IDEOLOGY

In its broadest and most impersonal way an ideology refers to an assortment of *ideas* reflecting the social needs and aspirations of an individual,

Orlo Strunk, Jr., received his STB from the Boston University School of Theology and his PhD in psychology and pastoral counseling from Boston University Graduate School. He is currently professor of psychology of religion at Boston University Graduate School of Arts and Sciences and is a psychologist and clinical supervisor at The Danielsen Institute, Boston University.

129

group, class, or culture. It is thus less than a full-blown, carefully arrived at Weltanschauung or world view, although it is part of that sort of "direction of striving" (Allport, 1937) or what Spranger (1923) long ago called "schemata of comprehensibility." Nor is a "way of being" as explicated by Carl Rogers (1980) equivalent to an ideology, although, as Rogers discovered in recent years, his person-centered approach has political content often associated with certain ideologies. The notions of personal values (Simmons, 1982) and value orientations (Lowe, 1969) are equally relevant in that they too carry with them power in relationships, including and especially those of a depthful nature. But values include an affective ingredient not necessarily present in an ideology. There are many other concepts which might be included in one's "proceptive dispositions" (Allport, 1961, pp. 265-266). Ideology is but one of these many "influences of set that intervene between sensory input and act." It is characterized by its cognitive character and its imbeddedness in a collective system or a meaning-sharing context.

DEFENSES AGAINST IDEOLOGICAL UNCOVERING

One of the major defenses against making manifest ideological propensities is that it tends to shatter mystique. Until the beginning of 20th-century science, medicine's mystique was undoubtedly its most potent healing force. With breakthroughs in medical research, the beginning of wholistic modes of thinking about health, and the growing participation of patients in determining the mode of healing, mystique has softened as a necessity. In many respects, certain kinds of contemporary psychotherapy emulate the more traditional medical stance, thus resisting the project of exposure of proceptive orientations, including ideologies.

Perhaps one of the most claimed reasons for not making manifest the therapist's ideologies is that psychotherapy is a science and thus stands clear of ideologies (Shilo, 1968). This certainly is one way of disclamation. Some of Freud's early musings echoed such an assumption. But with the development of modern psychotherapy—particularly those modes of therapy generated by Third Force Psychology and by the recognition that psychological studies are more accurately seen as humanities-related than as science—a new appreciation of the role of proceptive countertransference is beginning to take place. Part of this recognition is also manifested in the willingness to see the faith of the psychotherapist as playing some part in the psychotherapeutic process (Stern, 1981).

This recognition focuses on the ideology of the psychotherapist relative to his or her own notion of what psychotherapy is. In another place (Strunk, 1983), I have suggested that the failure to include this reality—particularly in not recognizing religion as a deviant reality system—can account for abortive therapeutic alliances. Proceptive dispositions constitute countertransference, or, perhaps more accurately, countertransference-like material (Lee, 1980). This massive and global set or orientation can be just as destructive or creative as those forces traditionally noted in the psychoanalytic literature as countertransference (Searles, 1979). Indeed, if one embraces such notions that an authentic therapeutic encounter is one in which "the *appeal* of a whole person can be answered only by the *presence* of a whole person" (van Kaam, 1966, p. 22), then the "fit" between therapist *as person* and client *as person* takes on considerable importance.

But exactly how such assumptive issues are made manifest is both problematic and complex. In the remaining part of this article, I would like to report on only one attempt to do this—*not,* however, because it has resolved the issue for one who *does* believe it essential to recognize ideological differences between therapist and client, but because experiences with it have demonstrated the reality of the phenomenon and the need to address it.

INFORMING THE CLIENT OF PSYCHOTHERAPY AS IDEOLOGY

Throughout the psychotherapeutic process ideological differences and ideological countertransference-like behavior may emerge and be handled in a variety of ways depending partly on the therapist's theoretical stance (e.g., Driscoll, 1984, pp. 81-83; Lee, 1980, pp. 107-133). Here, however, I am addressing the issue of ideological countertransference-like behavior as it may present itself in the initial contact with a client. Selection of this beginning phase of psychotherapy is based on two factors: (1) the observation that the assessment-alliance factors hold remarkable implications both in terms of immediate symptom relief as well as for long-term prognosis (Frank, 1978), and (2) the personal experience of discovering—at times after being far along on the psychotherapeutic journey—that my ideology of psychotherapy deviated capaciously from my client's.

In an attempt to confront this troublesome issue, I designed a professional card which contained a concise statement of my "notion" of what I believe personal psychotherapy is about. The 3-1/2-inch by 4-inch card is folded—the front half holding the typical information (degree, address, telephone number), the back half holding an appointment reminder. When the folded card is opened, the center space contains the following statement:

What is personal psychotherapy? It is a psychological process and journey aimed at alleviating your mental suffering and helping you to develop more effective ways of coping with conflict and stress.

Its long-term intentions are for you to achieve more personal integration and to move toward becoming the kind of person you wish to become.

What do you have a right to expect from me as your psychotherapist? You should expect me to be competent in my profession and to be a person you feel you can trust to share your personal concerns. You should be satisfied that I have completed the appropriate educational and training requirements; have obtained the proper state and/or national credentials; and that in our relationship my first concern will be you.

What do I have a right to expect of you as a client? Your desire for psychotherapy should be strong enough so that you will be present with me regularly as agreed upon, that you will meet your financial obligations as contracted, and that you will bring to our sessions materials for us to work together on (for instance, reports of current problems and feelings, relevant memories, dreams, images, drawings, writings, etc.).

Is there something we both have a right to expect? Although there are many qualities which help to form a good therapeutic relationship, there is one which is absolutely necessary: *Honesty.* Yours. Mine.

Following the first interview I give this card to the potential client indicating that she or he should read it carefully and that we will discuss it as part of our next interview when we will deal with contractual matters, particularly the issue of whether we feel comfortable enough with one another to continue in the therapeutic relationship.

As might be expected, this discussion often yields important information. A colleague who recently read this statement said, "But that's not at all my view of psychotherapy!" The enthusiasm of his response illustrated the reality of the differences in ideologies of psychotherapy which do indeed exist among psychotherapists. Clients, too, often have, and are willing to share, their differences, doubts, and agreements with the statement. One client explained, "Look, I was in therapy with a Rogerian for a year. What I need is advice!" As we explored this expectation, and as I related it to the client's history and presenting issues, we decided that the distance between our ideas about the nature of psychotherapy was so great that it would be best for both of us if we decided against seeing one another again.

On another occasion, a client tearfully reported, "You don't know how much talking about this means to me. I've been in therapy three times before; and I never knew what was expected of me. I do a lot of poetry writing, but I never dreamed my counselors were interested in seeing my poems."

Often the client will request elaboration of the statements:
"But I'm not sure what kind of person I wish to become."
"What does 'personal integration' mean?"
"Just how long a journey is this going to be?"
"Honesty isn't exactly my long suit."
"I think of the journey as a *spiritual* journey. Do you?"
I address directly these sort of comments in ways which allow both of us to clarify our assumptive differences and agreements.

Despite the fears usually expressed by colleagues relative to this approach, these early sessions rarely turn into intellectual discussions or philosophical dialogues. Mostly, clients understand the perspective and can compare it to their own understandings and expectations and can do so with ease and comfort. I try to make this phase of the interview flow with the larger issues of how psychotherapy might be able to help them in their life at this time and attempt to communicate the idea that there is no such thing as a single form of psychotherapy appropriate for everyone and for all problems and all journeys.

In this early encounter, I am not attempting to "diagnose" for a perfect fit but to set a fair impression of just how far apart or how close we are in our notions of what psychotherapy is, how it works, and what its limitations are.

Of course, this approach doesn't always work! Perhaps the greatest difficulty is the fact that frequently persons seeking therapy are so troubled that their tunnel vision prevents them from dealing with the question of "fit." They need help—*now* and from *anyone!* The ideological differences are so very secondary that they cannot be addressed with insight and in an authentic fashion. When this is the case, I do the best I can and do not belabor the point. But following each session I do continue to give my card to such clients as appointment reminders; and there have been times when such troubled persons have returned to the beliefs expressed on the card. On one such occasion, a client during her 16th hour paused in the midst of an especially difficult account, shook her head, and said, "No, that's not so. I've got to be honest. I remember—honesty."

Although this simple procedure contains many flaws and deals with only one aspect of proceptive countertransference-like phenomena—the ideologies of psychotherapy—it does indicate, I think, how it is possible to take a bit more seriously the realization that psychotherapy carries with it a recognition that when two persons meet and mutually agree to deal with issues of life, the traditional scientific object/subject paradigms need to be modified considerably, perhaps even laid aside. And one way to do this is to be open to the realities of our ideologies, to place them before the two of us as honestly as we can, and to deal with them as but one more important reality standing in need of examination, exploration, and consciousness expansion.

REFERENCES

Allport, G. W. (1961). *Pattern and growth in personality.* New York: Holt, Rinehart & Winston.

Driscoll, R. (1984). *Pragmatic psychotherapy.* New York: Van Nostrand Reinhold.

Ehrenwald, J. (Ed.). (1976). *The history of psychotherapy: From healing magic to encounter.* New York: Jason Aronson.

Frank, J. D. (1978). Expectation and therapeutic outcome—the placebo effect and the role of induction interview. In J. D. Frank, R. Hoehn-Saric, S. D. Imber, B. L. Liberman, & A. R. Stone, *Effective ingredients of successful psychotherapy.* New York: Brunner/Mazel.

Lee, R. R. (1980). *Cleary and clients: The practice of pastoral psychotherapy.* New York: The Seabury Press.

Lowe, C. M. (1969). *Value orientations in counseling and psychotherapy: The meanings of mental health.* San Francisco: Chandler Publishing Co.

Rogers, C. R. (1980). *A way of being.* Boston: Houghton Mifflin.

Searles, H. F. (1979). *Countertransference and related subjects.* New York: International Universities Press.

Shils, E. (1968). The concept and function of ideology. *International encyclopedia of the social sciences,* vol. 7(pp. 66-76). New York: The Macmillan Company and The Free Press.

Simmons, D. D. (1982). *Personal valuing: An introduction.* Chicago: Nelson-Hall.

Spranger, E. (1923). *Lebensformen.* Halls: Niemeyer.

Stern, E. M. (Ed.). (1981). *The other side of the couch: What therapists believe.* New York: The Pilgrim Press.

Strunk, O. Jr. (1983). Religion as deviant reality: The psychotherapeutic dilemma. *The Bulletin of the National Guild of Catholic Psychiatrists, 29,* 29-35.

van Kaam, A. (1966). *The art of existential counseling.* Wilkes-Barre, PA: Dimension Books.

Psychotherapy as a Religious Process:
A Historical Heritage

Hendrika Vande Kemp

While I have long been interested in the integration of psychology and religion, I was motivated to expound the historical roots of this enterprise by two fellow psychologists whose knowledge of it was obviously limited to (or focused on) the contemporary scene. The first of these, Reverend Harold Ellens, longtime executive secretary of the Christian Association for Psychological Studies, startled me severely when he announced at the 11th annual John G. Finch Symposium on integration at Fuller Theological Seminary that "much of the really creative and definitive material on the intersection of theology and psychology has been published since 1977" (Ellens, 1981, p. 6, emphasis mine). While this comment might be justified by the narrower definition of "integration" in use in our evangelical Christian circle, the second comment was even more startling. The psychologist wrote: "Carl G. Jung was the first therapist to write about integrating the psychological and the spiritual . . . But it was [Scott] Peck who first revealed that he integrated his spiritual beliefs into his professional, clinical work" (Simpkinson, 1983, p. 1).

As a matter of fact, the integration of psychology with the religious and spiritual has been an active enterprise ever since psychology established itself as an independent discipline in the mid-nineteenth century (Vande Kemp, 1984). Probably the earliest effort in this direction, the writing of "Christian psychologies," preceded the birth of psychotherapy by several decades (Beck, 1843/1877; Chambers, n.d.; Delitzsch, 1855/1867; Fletcher, 1912; House, 1913; Keyser, 1928; Laidlaw, 1879; Norlie, 1923; Penn-Lewis, 1900; Rauch, 1840; Stalker, 1914; Sutherland, 1874). Contemporary Christian personality theories are a continuation of this approach, which focused on the nature of persons from a Christian perspective. A second effort, more loosely "integrative," was the psychology of religion movement which flourished at the turn of the century and into the 1920s (Beit-Hallahmi, 1974; Gorsuch, 1984). The

Hendrika Vande Kemp received her PhD in clinical psychology from the University of Massachusetts/Amherst in 1977. Currently she is an associate professor of psychology at Fuller Theological Seminary, where she teaches family therapy, borderline personality theory, the history of psychology, and courses in the integration of psychology and theology.

first major effort of this sort also emerged in the mid-nineteenth century, under the title *Psychology and Theology* (Alliott, 1855), following an even earlier treatise on the religious roots of insanity (Brigham, 1835).

Overlapping chronologically with both of these movements was an emphasis on mental and spiritual healing, which has received considerable attention in the literature of Christianity, and is often traced back to the Old and New Testaments (Bromberg, 1975; Cutten, 1911; Dearmer, 1909; McNeil, 1951; Weatherhead, 1951). Beginning early in the 20th century, the well-known pastoral psychology movement also differentiated itself out of the tradition of "care" and "cure" of souls, incorporating insights and techniques from the literature on psychotherapy and personality theory (Holifield, 1983; Kemp, 1947).

Finally, we can isolate a tradition of "religious psychology," including a variety of efforts to incorporate religious insights into psychological theory. Here we can include contemporary theoretical efforts at integration and religious approaches to psychotherapy, including the more global emphasis on "spirituality" which is becoming popular. The major journals and institutions/organizations devoted to these efforts are summarized in Tables 1 and 2.

Table 1

INSTITUTIONS RELATED TO INTEGRATION

1905	The Guild of Health (London)[1]
	The Emmanuel Society (London)[1]
	The Emmanuel Movement (Boston)[1]
1910	Pine Rest Christian Hospital and Rehabilitation Services (Grand Rapids, MI)[2]
1915	The Guild of St. Raphael (Anglican)[1]
1923	Proposed founding of Institute of Religious Psychology (Theodore Schroeder)[3]
1930	Council for Clinical Training[4]
1936	Guild of Pastoral Psychology (London)[4]
	Founding of City Temple Psychological Clinic (London)[1]
	American Foundation of Religion and Psychiatry (Marble Collegiate Church)[6]
1937	Church of Scotland Committee on Psychology[4,5]
	Milton Abbey (Dorset, London)[1]
1937?	London Clinic of Religious Psychology[1]
1942	The Pines[5]
1944	The Churches Council on Healing (England)[1]
1944?	Institute for Spiritual Counsel and Psychological Treatment, the St. Luke's Foundation (Stockholm)[1]
1945	Mennonite Mental Health Services[2]
1946	The Methodist Society for Medical and Pastoral Practice (England)[4]
1948	Bethesda Hospital Association (Denver; earlier served tuberculosis patients)[2]
	Institute for Rankian Psychoanalysis (Dayton)[5]
1949	Institute of Medical Pathology and Mental Healing (Athens)[1]

Table 1, continued

1953	Foundation for the Advancement of Religious Psychology (Los Angeles/ Fritz Kunkel)[5]
1954?	Christian Association for Psychological Studies[6]
1955	Guild for Psychological Studies (San Francisco)[5]
	Academy of Religion and Mental Health[6]
1956	International Conference on Spiritual Therapy[6]
	Lumen Vitae International Commission of Religious Psychology[3, 5]
1959	The American Academy of Religious Therapists[6]
1964	Graduate School of Psychology/Fuller Theological Seminary[6]
1967	Association for Clinical Pastoral Education (merger of several agencies)[4]
1972	Institute of Religion and Health (merger of several agencies)[4, 6]
1977?	Institute of Christian Counseling (Mt. Pleasant, MI)[6]
1970s	American Association of Christian Counselors (Winnetka, IL)[6]
	The Psychological Studies Institute (Atlanta)[6]
	Rosemead Graduate School of Psychology/Biola University[6]
	New York Institute of Metapsychiatry[5]
1981	California Christian Institute (Melodyland)[6]

Notes
[1] Mental and spiritual (and physical) healing
[2] Christian mental health services
[3] Psychology of religion
[4] Pastoral psychology
[5] Religious psychology
[6] (Judeo) Christian psychology

Table 2

JOURNALS RELATED TO THE INTEGRATION OF PSYCHOLOGY AND RELIGION

1899//	Journal of Psychosophy (Toronto: School of Practical Psychosophy and Psychosophical Society)[3]
1904- 1915	The American Journal of Religious Psychology and Education/The Journal of Religious Psychology (edited by G. Stanley Hall)[3]
1908 1909	Psychotherapy: A Course of Reading in Sound Psychology, Sound Medicine and Religion (edited by W. P. Parker/Centre Publishing Co.)[1]
1937+	Inward Light: Journal of the Friends Conference on Religion and Psychology[1, 3, 6]
1947+	The Journal of Pastoral Care[4]
1950+	Pastoral Psychology[4]
1954- 1956	Journal of Psychotherapy as a Religious Process (Dayton: Institute for Rankian Psychoanalysis)[5, 6]
1961+	Journal for the Scientific Study of Religion (Society for the Scientific Study of Religion)[3]
1961+	Journal of Religion and Health (Academy of Religion and Mental Health)[5, 6]
1963+	Insight: Quarterly Review of Religion and Mental Health (edited by Fintan McNamee)[6]

Table 2, continued

1966+	Journal of Pastoral Counseling (Iona College/Graduate Division of Pastoral Counseling)[4]
1971+	Psychologists Interested in Religious Issues Newsletter (American Psychological Association)
1973+	Journal of Psychology and Theology (Rosemead Graduate School of Psychology)[2, 3, 4, 6]
1976+	Journal of Psychology and Judaism[4, 6]
1977	Journal of Christian Counseling (The Institute of Christian Counseling)[2, 6]
1978+	International Forum for Logotherapy[5]
1982+	Journal of Psychology and Christianity (Christian Association for Psychological Studies)[3, 6]

Notes

[1] Mental and spiritual (and physical) healing

[2] Christian mental health service   [3] Psychology of religion

[4] Pastoral psychology   [5] Religious psychology

[6] (Judeo) Christian psychology

DEFINITIONS

While religion in many of these discussions connotes traditional Judaism, Protestantism, and Catholicism, many authors use it more broadly. It may be helpful to keep in mind its original denotation: "The main root of the term 'religion' is the Latin term *ligare,* from which our terms 'ligament' and 'ligature' come. Thus, *re-ligion* means, literally, a reconnection, reunion, reconciliation" (Mowrer, 1966, p. 37).

"Psychotherapy" has changed considerably in its connotation since its early use at the turn of the century. *The Oxford English Dictionary* (1933) shows it as a derivative of "psychotherapeutist," one who treats disease by psychic methods. Originally this denoted primarily treatment by sleep, suggestion, or hypnotism, as did C. L. Tuckey's (1889) book of that title, *Psychotherapeutics; or, treatment by sleep and suggestion.* By 1905 the term had also come to denote mind healing and faith healing, at least in the popular literature. Richard Cabot (1909), in a review of the literature on psychotherapy during the first decade of the 20th century, differentiated three groups within its ranks. In the "gaseous" or unreliable category he included New Thought, Christian Science, and related movements which "tend to say what is pleasant regardless of truth" (p. 18). In the "solid" category, which says "what is true regardless of the pleasure or of any other effect it may produce upon the hearer" (p. 18), he included the work of Janet, Breuer, Freud, Jung, and the Frenchmen Camus and Cagniez. In the "fluid" middle group, adapted to the general reader, he placed Paul Dubois (Professor of Psychotherapy at the University of

Berne), Hugo Munsterberg, Luther Gulick, Joseph Jastrow, Herman Oppenheim, Walton, Alfred T. Schofield, J. M. Bramwell, and the Emmanuel group: Elwood Worcester, Samuel McComb, and Isador Coriat (Worcester, McComb & Coriat, 1980).

PSYCHOTHERAPY AS SOUND PSYCHOLOGY, SOUND MEDICINE, AND SOUND RELIGION

One of the first explicitly integrative efforts in the United States was the movement of moral and religious reeducation for functional disorders begun at Emmanuel Church in Boston (Worcester et al., 1908) and extended to churches in Chicago, Rochester, Cambridge, Northampton, Waltham, Newark, Detroit, Buffalo, Brooklyn, and a number of smaller cities. Followers of this movement launched a short-lived journal, *Psychotherapy: A Course of Reading in Sound Psychology, Sound Medicine, and Sound Religion,* of which 12 numbers were published in 1908 and 1909. Psychotherapy was defined by the editor as "the attempt to help the sick through mental, moral and spiritual methods" (Parker, 1908, p. i). W. B. Parker, in his editorial, aimed to clarify for the journal's readers "what is the essential truth of the various healing movements" and to increase their "mental and spiritual resources" (p. i). "Psychotherapy" included the Christian healing tradition, and the journal featured a historical section including surveys of healing in the Old Testament, the New Testament, the Early Church, the Middle Ages, and the Reformation. It also relied on the scientific knowledge of medicine and physiological psychology, featuring contributions by John E. Donley, Frank K. Hallock, Beatrice M. Hinkle, Charles L. Tuckey, George L. Meylan, Richard Newton, Frederick Peterson, James J. Putnam, and Richard C. Cabot (who was instrumental in the later establishment of Clinical Pastoral Education [Holifield, 1983]); and the psychologists James R. Angell, Joseph Jastrow, Josiah Royce, and Robert S. Woodworth. A number of pastors also contributed, describing their local parish experiences with "psychotherapy" in the Emmanuel tradition. As described by one pastor (Powell, 1908), psychotherapy proceeded as follows:

> The patient is subjected to a searching inquiry into every circumstance touching in any respect upon the mental or physical condition. The failure to reply with perfect frankness invariably closes the discussion and makes treatment utterly impossible. Nothing is spared to secure the patient's confidence, and to establish the closest spiritual relationship. Directions are given in regard to mental and spiritual hygiene, and a course of reading is mapped out, sometimes covering a period of weeks. In a few instances the frank discussion

and the daily reading of the books suggested have been the largest
factors in the patient's forward march to health. (p. 89)

A major question discussed in the journal's pages was the role of the
clergy and religion in psychotherapy. The Reverend Charles Place (1908)
applied psychotherapy to neurasthenias and psychasthenias, but excluded
phobias, fears, and fixed ideas. In treatment, he felt that the minister
"desires to reach back through the nervous symptoms to their causes in
the mind or soul" (p. 82). Prayer was also regarded as powerful in the re-
quisite education of the will. The Reverend Dickinson Miller (1908) went
even further in his assertion that "religion, regarded scientifically and
from without, is psychotherapy . . . . It is the relief of souls, and
ministers through the whole soul to the whole vitality by allaying unrest
and restoring confidence" (pp. 35, 43). The Reverend Cameron Davis
(1909), in his treatment of "weak character," noted that a simple application of the principles stated in the Sermon on the Mount was vital in the
reeducation and spiritualizing of souls (p. 75). Richard Cabot (1909)
delineated the minister's role in psychotherapy as the "task of spiritual
and moral education" (p. 11). While Cabot did not feel ministers should
treat organic disease, he deplored the censure and condemnation of the
Emmanuel Movement by physicians. Similarly, James Jackson Putnam,
cited in the editor's notes to Cabot's article, focused the minister's task on
"the development of character and motives" (p. 17).

Hugo Münsterburg (1909), an eminent psychologist writing on psychotherapy, felt that the conjunction of psychotherapy and religion should
form a transitional stage, leading to a time when "the ministerial function
is confined to the spiritual task of upbuilding a mind while the therapeutic
function remains entirely in the hands of the physician" (p. 346). Münsterburg felt that the analytic task of the psychologist was incompatible
with the synthetic task of the minister. Whether or not Münsterburg was
correct in his assumptions, a differentiation of functions did occur. By
1930, a tradition of pastoral psychology had clearly differentiated itself
(in task, if not in theory) from the psychotherapeutic tradition of psychologists and psychiatrists (Holifield, 1983; Vande Kemp, 1984).

A CONTESTED DIVORCE

This separation of religious and therapeutic process was not without
challenges, even during its early years. Carl Jung's (1933) interest in
religion has been well documented as has Freud's correspondence with
the Reverend Oskar Pfister, a pastor in the Reformed Church (Freud &
Pfister, 1963). Less well known is the interaction between Alfred Adler
and the Reverend Ernst Jahn, a Lutheran whose interest in psychotherapy

focused on its potential contribution to the "cure of souls." They co-authored a volume (Adler & Jahn, 1933) which included Jahn's essay, "The psychotherapy of Christianity," Adler's response, and Jahn's closing comments. Adler's response is revealing, as it evidences awareness of numerous attempts to integrate individual psychology with religious principles, most of which he criticizes. Oskar Pfister he accused of "disordered thinking" in his critique of individual psychology as too humanistic; the Catholic Rudolf Allers he took to task for not attempting to make "psychological anthropology" a part of the Christian ministry, and for making it more palatable by translating it into ministerial terminology. Fritz Künkel, who founded the Foundation of Religious Psychology, he regarded as inappropriate in introducing the concept of contrition into psychotherapy; Arvid Runestam, who authored a "moral" critique of psychoanalysis, he chastised for locating the origin of neurosis in the repression of the religious striving by the indulgences of the drives.

Adler himself clearly regarded individual psychology as a form of, or equivalent to, religion. It was religious in that it subordinated all other efforts to the ultimate goal of ideal community and the strengthening of social interest. Thus, Adler definitely regarded psychotherapy as a religious process.

Others also pointed to religion as a therapeutic process, emphasizing the positive contributions of religion. One such writer was Gordon Allport, whose interest in religion was evident even in his earliest work, the classic text on *Personality* (1937), where he stated that "psychotherapy recognizes [the] integrative function of religion in personality, soundness of mind being aided by the possession of a completely embracing theory of life" (p. 226). In a later paper (1944) he stated that "the person who directs his attention to his religious quest usually finds therapy along the way—unexpectedly" (p. 29). Allport emphasized the importance of religious assessment in the process of diagnosis (1937, p. 393), an emphasis echoed by Alphonse Maeder (1944/1953). Maeder stressed that "the beginning of spiritual development may arise during a purely psychologically oriented treatment" (p. 158). In addition to stressing the importance of the spiritual element in psychotherapy, Maeder pointed out "that among religious patients there has been an increase in the number who wish to visit only a psychotherapist who has religious faith" (p. 181), attesting to their awareness of a spiritual component in psychotherapy.

That the intertwining of psychology and religion reflects an essential fact of human nature is summarized in the recent literature by James Hillman (1975):

> Our psychologizing may seem actually a theologizing, and this book as much a work of theology as of psychology. In a way this is and

must be so, since the merging of psychology and religion is less the confluence of two different streams than the result of their single source—the soul. The psyche itself keeps psychology and religion bound to each other. (p. 167)

PSYCHOTHERAPY AS A RELIGIOUS PROCESS

One of the first explicit efforts at integration following the differentiation of psychotherapy from pastoral care was the *Journal of Psychotherapy as a Religious Process,* published by the Institute for Rankian Psychoanalysis (IRP) in Dayton, Ohio. Under the guidance of the Reverend William Rickel, a trained social worker, IRP offered training in Christian psychoanalysis, asserting ''that all personality and neurotic difficulties begin in the soul of man and not in the body or mind'' (as stated on the cover of Volume 3 of the *Journal*). Rickel and his colleagues owed their inspiration to Otto Rank, especially his book *Beyond Psychology* (1939), where Rank stated that ''man is born beyond psychology and he dies beyond it, but he can *live* beyond it only through vital experience of his own—in religious terms, through revelation, conversion or rebirth'' (p. 16). Rickel's first (1954a) editorial asserted ''that psychotherapy is, from the practitioner's point of view, a religious ministration and, from the patient's angle, an experience of rebirth'' (p. 2). He regarded psychotherapy as a ''moral, ethical, and valuational experience'' (1954b, p. 68), leading to moral responsibility. Rickel is particularly interesting in that his theological training *followed* his training in social work. For contemporary Christian psychotherapists the reverse order is much more typical.

While Rickel's journal experienced a quick demise, it attracted the interests of a number of clinicians who later became well known as ''integrationists.'' One of the most significant of these was Paul Tournier (1954), the eminent Swiss psychiatrist. Tournier described four situations where psychotherapy becomes soul-healing: when the patient expresses a sense of responsibility and makes a confession; when the transference leads the patient to devotion to Christ; when self-examination leads the patient to repentance and openness to God's grace; and when psychotherapy leads to exploration of existential questions. Another contributor was Wilfred Daim (1955), a member of the Vienna Working Circle for Depth Psychology, who based his psychotherapy on the assumption that the roots of neurosis were ''found in the idolization of a relative object . . . the normal tendency of acknowledging the true absolute—the transcendent God—is repressed and something relative is endowed with absolute character'' (pp. 25-26). Thus, the psychoanalytic process must always be a ''process of salvation'' (p. 35). Count Igor Caruso (1955), a

Catholic who founded the Vienna Circle, reflected a similar perspective, regarding neurosis as an *existential heresy:* The person is fixated at a period which obstructs mature harmony *in the world of values* (p. 6). Caruso also regarded psychotherapy as a "religious process," in that "religious experience is a way of knowing more perfect than others" (p. 21), while denouncing "the spiritualistic propaganda" of the logotherapist (p. 6). More explicitly Christian in his assertion was Alphonse Maeder (1955), a follower of the Oxford Group Movement who regarded psychotherapy as "the purest form of spiritual surgery" (p. 40) in which God's grace is essential.

Charles Baudoin (1956), Privat-Dozent at the University of Geneva, echoed in his contribution the insights of Jung:

> I have been struck like-wise—I would not presume to say by the identity—by the singular relationship between the conclusions of psychological healing and those of spiritual aspiration. I understand, in one way or another, the same cry of anguish of the "creature separated," the same search for unity and union—the quest of the Grail—. (p.29)

A final major contributor was Roberto Assagioli (1956), Director of the Institute for Psychosynthesis in Rome. His emphasis was on "the nervous conditions appearing at the various stages of spiritual realization" (p. 31). Assagioli clearly differentiated between persons needing personal psychosynthesis and those needing spiritual psychosynthesis—"an alignment between the soul and the personality" (p. 45).

While support for Rickel's journal was high on the continent, as indicated by both article contributions and letters, such support was not forthcoming in the United States. Rickel's ideas were received by major pastoral counselors very negatively (Rickel et al., 1956). The theologian Paul Tillich (Rickel et al., 1956) of Harvard felt that Rickel disregarded psychological fixations, belonging in the realm of psychiatry, and accused him of mystical perfectionism" (p. 40). Psychiatrist John Millet of the American Rehabilitation Committee, felt Rickel too quickly became "the champion of the priest as opposed to the physician" (p. 42). The Reverend Russell Dicks of Duke University Divinity School felt the distinction between psychotherapy and pastoral care *must* be maintained, on the grounds that "the emotionally mature understand deep theology; the emotionally ill need depth therapy" (p. 46). And even Anton Boisen, founder of Clinical Pastoral Education and champion of the integrative value of both religious and psychotic experiences, stated: "I am of the opinion that few psychiatrists have any understanding of the religious factors in mental illness and few ministers are equipped to deal with morbid mental states" (p. 46).

For a variety of reasons, Rickel decided to discontinue the journal and left Dayton for an extended stay in Europe. One reason was the lack of suitable material without a Jungian emphasis. Ironically, two major integrative books had appeared during the *Journal's* short life. The first was W. Earl Biddle's (1955) *Integration of Psychiatry and Religion,* the first book to use the term "integration" in this context. Biddle asserted that "there is a basic religious element underlying all neurotic and psychotic disorders, though it is not very obvious . . . When frustrations impede progress toward the Supreme Being, then some type of mental disorder becomes evident" (p. 8). Biddle's book, offering a Freudian perspective, was popular enough to be reprinted in a paperback edition in 1962. The second book was Harry Guntrip's *Mental health and the cure of souls* (1956), published in the United States as *Psychotherapy and religion* (1957). Guntrip, a psychotherapist who had previous experience as a pastoral counselor and Congregational minister, presented the object-relational perspective. Like Allport, he regarded religion as a major therapeutic force:

> Psychotherapy is evidently a truly religious experience and religion at its maturest is the fullest attainment of the aims of psychotherapy. Whether religious experience can penetrate into the unconscious depths of the personality in the way the psychoanalytical psychotherapy can do, is a matter for factual investigation. I would be prepared to say that a sound and enlightened religious faith and some capacity for religious experience in spite of personality disturbances provides the best and most helpful setting for psychotherapy. (p. 199)

CONCLUSIONS

It is clear from reviewing the literature that the intimate connection between psychotherapy and religion has always been evident to at least a minority of psychotherapists and religious professionals. Some among them recognized the therapeutic value of religious faith. Others recognized that a dimension could be added to the pastoral care of souls by introducing the techniques and insights of psychotherapy. Still others simply recognized that the spiritual and psychological were artificial distinctions, impossible to maintain in professional practice. Thus, contemporary psychotherapists who seek to serve the religiously committed client can turn to a rich tradition for guidance and direction, and for a clear articulation of the issue. Perhaps we can bring to fruition the seeds planted by these early integrators, restoring wholeness to the divided soul.

REFERENCES

Adler, A. & Jahn, E. (1933). *Religion and Individualpsychologie: Eine prinzipielle Auseinander-setzung uber Menschenfunrung.* London: Jackson & Walford. Vienna: R. Passer.

Alliott, R. (1855). *Psychology and theology; or, Psychology applied to the investigation of questions relating to religion, natural theology, and revelation.* London: Jackson & Walford.

Allport, G. W. (1937). *Personality: A psychological interpretation.* New York: Henry Holt & Company.

Allport, G. W. (1944). *The roots of religion. Advent paper no. 1.* Boston: Editorial Board Advent Papers.

Assagioli, R. (1956). Spiritual development and nervous disease. *Journal of Psychotherapy as a Religious Process, 3,* 30-40. (Originally published in *The Hibbert Journal,* 1937.)

Baudoin, C. (1956). Unity and communion. *Journal of Psychotherapy as a Religious Process, 3,* 6-29.

Beck, J. T. (1877). *Outlines of biblical psychology.* Edinburgh: T. & T. Clark. (Original German edition, 1843.)

Beit-Hallahmi, B. (1974). Psychology of religion 1880-1930: The rise and fall of a psychological movement. *Journal of the History of the Behavioral Sciences, 10*(4), 84-90.

Biddle, W. E. (1955). *Integration of religion and psychiatry.* New York: Macmillan.

Brigham, A. (1835). *Observations on the influence of religion upon the health and physical welfare of mankind.* Boston: Marsh, Capen, & Lyon.

Bromberg, W. (1975). *From shaman to psychotherapist: A history of the treatment of mental illness.* Chicago: H. Regnery.

Cabot, R. C. (1909). The literature of psychotherapy. *Psychotherapy: A Course of Reading in Sound Psychology, Sound Medicine, and Sound Religion, 3*(4), 18-25.

Cabot, R. C. (1909). Whose business is psychotherapy? *Psychotherapy: A Course of Reading in Sound Psychology, Sound Medicine, and Sound Religion, 3* (40), 5-12.

Caruso, I. A. (1955). Personalistic psychoanalysis and symbolic knowledge. *Journal of Psychotherapy as a Religious Process, 2,* 2-23.

Chambers, O. (n.d.). *Biblical psychology: A series of preliminary studies.* 2nd ed. London: Simpkin Marshall.

Cutten, G. B. (1911). *Three thousand years of mental healing.* New York: Scribner's.

Daim, W. (1955). Depth psychology and salvation. *Journal of Psychotherapy as a Religious Process, 2,* 24-37.

Davis, C. J. (1909). The Emmanuel Movement at Trinity Church, Buffalo. *A Course of Reading in Sound Psychology, Sound Medicine and Sound Religion. 3,*(2), 72-75.

Dearmer, P. (1909). *Body and soul; An inquiry into the effects of religion upon health, with a description of Christian works of healing, from the New Testament to the present day.* New York: E. P. Dutton.

Delitzsch, F. J. (1867). *A System of biblical psychology.* (R. E. Wallis, Tr.) Edinburgh: T & T Clark. (Original German edition, 1855.)

Ellens, J. H. (1981). *God's grace and human health. II. Implications for psychology theory development.* The John G. Finch Lectures, Fuller Theological Seminary, Pasadena, CA.

Fletcher, M. S. (1912). *The psychology of the New Testament.* 2nd ed. London: Hodder & Stoughton.

Freud, S. & Pfister, O. (1963). *Psychoanalysis and faith: The letters of Sigmund Freud and Oskar Pfister.* H. Meng & E. L. Freud (Eds.), (E. Mosbacher, Tr.). New York: Basic Books.

Gorsuch, R. (1984). Measurement: the boon and bane of investigating religion. *American Psychologist, 39*(3), 228-236.

Guntrip, H. (1956). *Mental health and the cure of souls.* London: Independent Press. Also published (1957) as *Psychotherapy and religion.* New York: Harper & Brothers.

Hillman, J. (1975). *Re-visioning psychology.* New York: Harper & Row.

Holifield, E. B. (1938). *A history of pastoral care in America: From salvation to self-realization.* Nashville: Abingdon.

House, E. L. (1913). *The psychology of orthodoxy.* New York: Fleming H. Revell.

Jung, C. G. (1933). *Modern man in search of a soul.* (W. S. Dell & C. F. Bayness, Tr.). New York: Harcourt, Brace & World.

Kemp, C. F. (1947). *Physicians of the soul: A history of pastoral counseling.* New York: Macmillan.

Keyser, L. S. (1928). *A handbook of Christian psychology.* Burlington, Iowa: The Lutheran Literary Board.

Laidlaw, J. (1879). *The Bible doctrine of man; or, the anthropology and psychology of scripture.* Edinburgh: T. & T. Clark.

Maeder, A. (1953). *Ways to psychic healing* (T. Lit, Tr.). New York: Charles Scribner's Sons. (Original German edition, 1944.)

Maeder, A. (1955). A new concept of the psychotherapist's role. *Journal of Psychotherapy as a Religious Process, 2,* 38-46.

McNeill, J. T. (1951). *A history of the cure of souls.* New York: Harper & Brothers.

Miller, D. S. (1908). What religion has to do with psychotherapy. *Psychotherapy: A Course of Reading in Sound Psychology, Sound Medicine, and Sound Religion, 1*(3), 35-51.

Mowrer, O. H. (1966). Abnormal reactions or actions? (An autobiographical answer.) Dubuque: Wm. C. Brown.

Munsterburg, H. (1909). *Psychotherapy.* New York: Moffat, Yard, & Co.

Norlie, O. M. (1923). *An elementary Christian psychology: A general psychology from a Christian viewpoint.* Minneapolis: Augsburg.

Parker, W. P. (1908). Announcement. *Psychotherapy: A Course of Reading in Sound Psychology, Sound Medicine, and Sound Religion, 1*(1), i-vi.

Penn-Lewis, J. (1900). *Soul and spirit: A glimpse into Bible psychology.* Leicester: The Overcomer Book Room.

Place, A. (1908). The clergyman's part in psychotherapy. *Psychotherapy: A Course of Reading in Sound Psychology, Sound Medicine, and Sound Religion, 1*(1), 81-85.

Powell, P. (1908). Psychotherapy at Northamptom: An account of personal experience. *Psychotherapy: A Course of Reading in Sound Psychology, Sound Medicine, and Sound Religion, 1*(1), 87-95.

Psychotherapeutics. (1933). *The Oxford English Dictionary. Vol. III.* Oxford: Claredon Press, 1553.

Rank, O. (1939). *Beyond psychology.* New York: Dover Publications.

Rauch, F. A. (1840). *Psychology; or, a view of the human soul: Including anthropology.* New York: M. W. Dodd.

Rickel, W. (1954). Editorial. *Journal of Psychotherapy as a Religious Process, 1*(2), 96-108.

Rickel, W. (1954). Psychotherapy as moral growth. *Journal of Psychotherapy as a Religious Process, 1,* 67-84.

Rickel, W., Tillich, P., Wise, C. A., Millet, J. A. P., Dicks, R. A. and Boison, A. T. (1956). Readers' forum: Is psychotherapy a religious process? *Pastoral Psychology, 7*(62), 36-46.

Simpkinson, C. H. (1983). Psychiatrist Scott Peck: On the road less traveled. *The Common Boundary between Spirituality and Psychotherapy, 1*(4), 1-2.

Stalker, J. (1914). *Christian psychology.* New York: Hodder & Stoughton.

Sutherland, G. (1874). *Christian psychology: a new exhibition of the capacities and faculties of the human spirit, investigated and illustrated from the Christian standpoint.* Sidney: William Maddock.

Tuckey, C. L. (1889). *Psychotherapeutics; or, treatment by sleep and suggestion.*

Tournier, P. (1954). The frontier between psychotherapy and soul-healing. *Journal of Psychotherapy as a Religious Process, 1,* 12-21.

Vande Kemp, H., with Malony, H. N. (1984). *Psychology and theology in western thought 1672-1965: A historical and annotated bibliography.* Millwood, NY: Kraus International Publications.

Weatherhead, L. (1951). *Psychology, religion and healing. A critical study of all the non-physical methods of healing, with an examination of the principles underlying them and the techniques employed to express them, together with some conclusions regarding further investigation and action in this field.* London: Hodder & Stoughton.

Worcester, E., McComb, S., & Coriat, I. H. (1908). *Religion and medicine: The moral control of nervous disorders.* New York: Moffatt, Yard, and Co.

Initial Encounters
of Religious and Priests
with Psychotherapy

Ann Marie Wallace

The monumental change in our times precipitated by global cultural shifts affects everything and everyone, including the Roman Catholic Church, as well as the religious men and women, and diocesan priests (see Appendix) who are committed to it in special lifestyles. Such change affects people in ways that are shared by many but also in ways that are unique to specific cultures and institutions. This article is an attempt to identify some issues priests and religious bring to psychotherapy, some of which are related to their life-styles. Because of the paucity of recent professional literature in this area, an interview format was chosen. Seven therapists were interviewed whose clients were either exclusively or predominantly religious and priests. They were identified as particularly knowledgeable in this area through reputation, workshops, and professional writing. The interviews were limited to psychotherapists who were Roman Catholic, five of whom were religious themselves. They are located in the Midwest, the South, and the Northeast and have from 8 to 19 years of experience.

BACKGROUND

Following is a somewhat simplistic but perhaps useful sketch of some aspects of religious life before and after the Second Vatican Council which concluded in 1965. It provides a context for the responses to the in-

Ann Marie Wallace received her PhD in counseling and school psychology from Fordham University in 1963. She is director of the Division of Counseling and Community Services at Fairfield University, Fairfield, Connecticut.

This article is a synthesis of the interview responses of the following psychotherapists whose cooperation and assistance is gratefully acknowledged:

Benedict J. Groeschel, OFMCap, Director, Office of Spritual Development, Archdiocese of New York; William F. Kraft, Carlow College; James B. Lloyd, CSP, Director, Graduate Division of Pastoral Counseling, Iona College; Sheila M. Murphy, Canton College; Susan Roth, OSB, Paschal House, Archdiocese of New Orleans; Sean D. Sammon, FMS, International Clinical Director, House of Affirmation, Boston, MA; James R. Zullo, FSC, Director, Christian Brothers Counseling and Consultation Center, Westchester, Ill.

terviews. Priests and religious are people, that is, human beings like everyone else with the same potential for growth, creativity, fulfillment, and integration but also with the same weaknesses, limitations, needs, drives, fears, and anxieties. This may seem like a strange statement, but for many Catholics, and even for priests and religious themselves, this is a rather recent "discovery." In the pre-Vatican II Church, priests and religious were viewed in terms of their specialness. They were a people set apart, dedicated and consecrated by vows (see Appendix) to God and to the Church. Because of the focus on their "sacredness" they were expected to be perfect, or at least much better than lay people, and to present this image to others.

There were decided advantages and disadvantages to being a priest or religious in this Church. The individual's identity, meaning system, and relevance were rather clear and well defined, supported by the admiration, respect, and esteem of the laity. For the religious, the life-style in the local community (see Appendix) was highly structured with unambiguous rules about friendships and recreation. There were few questions about ministry (see Appendix) in religious congregations, (see Appendix) with some in fact identified exclusively with one or a few within the Church. People were said to enter a "teaching" order or a "nursing" order. Priests and religious lived primarily for the Church or the congregation they joined. There were limitations, however, for some people. The individuality of the person suffered. Autonomy and decision making about one's life were almost nonexistent; affective development was limited or repressed. Close relationships were considered hindrances to the spiritual life. The energies and talents of the person were often limited to a specific type of work or need of the order whether the person was suited to it or not.

The developed understanding of the Church and of religious life and the priesthood since the Vatican Council has opened the door for significant and far-reaching changes in the lives of priests and religious. While both life-styles are still regarded as special modes of dedication and consecration to God and the Church, much of the security that came from the clarity of rule, structure, and ministry, along with the unquestioned support of the laity are gone. Many priests and religious have, or are moving to, a greater appreciation of their human nature as being both the gifted and flawed, one we all share. They are priests or religious, not because they are better than others, but because in some mysterious way they perceive an inner invitation from Christ to "Follow Me" (Matthew 9:19) in this particular life-style. Like everyone else, the journey toward wholeness or integration of the true self involves facing the contents of what Freud called the id or Jung the shadow—a painful experience at best. As priests and religious, their commitment invites them not only to human growth and development but to a life of spiritual transformation, a transcending goal referred to as union with God. This also involves facing the darkness within oneself as the mystics have pointed out. In their struggle for psychospiritual development and transformation, some reach an impasse and need the help of a therapist to deal with psychological issues which are either blocking psychospiritual growth or need to be integrated into their value systems.

INTERVIEWS

To help practicing psychotherapists deepen their understanding of priests and religious today, the responses to the following questions are reported as synthesized from the interviews.

How Do Priests and Religious Come Into Therapy?

All psychotherapists report that the vast majority are self-referred. Many of them have discussed their current personal situation with a close friend, a friend who has been or is currently in therapy, a superior or a bishop and have come with their encouragement and support. These clients are highly motivated, intelligent, articulate, and move quickly in therapy. Some are referred by a bishop or superior. The experiences of the therapists differ. Twenty percent of one therapist's clients come this way. He finds that they are anxious for help and offer little resistance. The others have far fewer such referrals. Some therapists find that these clients come with such anger and resistance that they simply terminate until they are ready. Other therapists will work with them for one or two sessions, giving them the freedom to go or stay, even providing the names of other therapists. Many stay once the choice is theirs. Some initially present the problem as belonging to others: they don't understand, they are unfair, won't listen, and so forth, and are able eventually to work through to their own personality problems.

Since the Cost of Therapy for Priests and Religious Is Frequently Underwritten by the Bishop or by the Religious Order, Are There Any Implications With Regard to Confidentiality?

All the therapists interviewed make it very clear that the contract is between the therapist and the client, not the religious order or diocese. Should the superior or bishop wish a report, it is given only with the written consent of the client who works with the therapist on the content and, if written, receives a copy. In most instances, such communications are handled in a three-way session. In the case of suicidal ideation, therapists would notify the superior or a friend who lives with the client if they

thought the situation warranted it. In the rare instances when this has occurred, psychiatric referral and medication were sought.

Therapists vary on the issue of accountability. Some see it as belonging
to the domain of the client who is responsible to the superior and to the
community. A conjoint session with the provincial and the therapist may
be part of this understanding of accountability. Other therapists take the
responsibility for it on themselves in that they will confront the unmo-
tivated client and move to a mutually agreed upon termination. In increasingly rare instances, at the end of an administration in the congregation,
or at the beginning of a new one, provincials will refer people who have
been "problems" for 20 to 30 years and "something should be done."
The prognosis may be limited. One therapist will indicate this to the referring superior after diagnosis to remove false hopes. There is no sharing of
specific information with the superior, nor is the client informed because
the therapist deemed it too discouraging at that time for someone who had
taken such a big step.

Have You Noticed Anything Significant in the Development of the Therapeutic Relationship With Priests and Religious Regarding Trust or Other Issues?

Most seem to establish the relationship and develop trust fairly easily.
The therapists attribute this to the reputations they have established
through other clients. Such clients see priests as especially bound by the
"seal of the Confessional" and some, where there is a mixed staff, will
request a priest-therapist. It takes longer to work through the trust issue
with clients whose confidentiality has been violated in the past. Transference issues come up in terms of authority figures, or images such as big
brother or big sister, coach, or parent. When the therapist is also a religious, the superior figure can also surface.

Some therapists had experience with the issue of obedience which
enters many authority relationships for priests and religious. Some view
the therapist as the superior checking up to see how well they are keeping
the rules. Others want directives they can carry out and so avoid the
therapeutic process entirely. This is handled very well in residential settings where the other clients confront it quickly. It is not a major issue,
however. Some religious may enter therapy because of obedience to the
superior. Since most superiors are quite aware that they cannot "force"
therapy, they accept early termination if there is no motivation.

Have You Observed Anything Significant About the Ages of Priests and Religious Who Come to Therapy?

The age range across the board is from the early 20s to the 80s. Most
find their clients concentrated in one or two age ranges with smaller numbers elsewhere. The majority are reported to be in the middle range, but

the definition of this range varies. One therapist reported an almost total clientele from 35 to 45 years, and one a bi-modal distribution with one concentration in the late 20s and the other from the early to late 40s. Two reported differing ranges for women and men with the women entering therapy earlier. The men ranged from the 40s to the 60s with fewer in the 60s. For the women, one range was from the 30s to the 50s and the other was from the 30s to the early 40s only.

What Are the Presenting Problems in Therapy That Might Be Considered Unique to This Group?

At the core, the problems are no different from those of the population in general. Because of the unique life-style of the priest and religious, however, the manifestations and resolutions of the issues may differ. A number of the presenting problems cluster around interpersonal relationships which touch off concern about getting along in community, having no friends, intimacy, male-female relationships in ministry and friendship, sexuality and sexual behavior, discovering and dealing with one's affective self, the experience of dissatisfaction and emptiness in community life, conflict management, and explosiveness in community. Other issues center around self-esteem and self-worth because of a poor self-image and are related to issues of guilt, perfectionism, feeling unappreciated, feeling like a cog in a wheel, and changing male-female roles and identity. A third area relates to ministry and may involve the desire to redirect one's energies to a new ministry or may simply be the problem of workaholism.

The religious order as an institution raises issues of concern about staying or leaving, relationships with major superiors, mourning and disillusionment over the death of religious life as it was, or not being able to get what one wants from community life. Others come because they have lost the sense of the spiritual dimension to their lives and felt they were working at jobs like lay people. Some have somatic complaints while others speak of a sense of unrest or feelings of mild depression.

Have You Observed Any Differences in the Issues Presented by Religious Men, Religious Women, and Diocesan Priests?

Most respondents saw more similarities than differences although some did emerge. Religious women expressed concern about interpersonal relationships in community and bonding with others, were searching for an identity not defined by the congregation or their work, wanted to learn about their affective dimension and integrate it, and experienced conflict in ministry where they received little recognition for the work done as compared with priests. Some were looking at the state of their congregations and wondering about remaining. Some therapists noted that women manifested a mild depression in midlife while one identified obesity and spending money as symptoms of conflict or negative emotions.

Religious men see issues of relationship in terms of community, getting along, handling explosiveness, anger, getting in touch with the affective and integrating it, sexuality, intimacy, and the changing male image in Church and society. Diocesan priests raised issues of relationship in terms of intimacy, spoke of loneliness, lack of community and support systems, the lack of ongoing formation, burnout and workaholism, cynicism and frustration, friendships with men and women, the changing male image, affectivity, anger, sexuality and sexual behavior, and struggles with celibacy which some see as part of the package for priesthood and not a call for them. One therapist who works exclusively with male religious and priests found no difference in the issues they raised. He did find that the religious priest has greater opportunities for variety in ministry and for living situations whereas diocesan priests are limited almost exclusively to parish work and rectory living where, in a sense, they "live over the store." Because of smaller numbers, the religious superior is more sensitive to the needs of the individual than are diocesan authorities.

What Are the Issues of the Young Adult Religious?

Those in their early 20s are in formation. Some have raised issues of authority, disillusionment with religious life, or are looking at their personalities to see if they are compatable with community living. Others are working their way into religious life and are dealing with the ordinary issues of personal struggles and interpersonal relationships. They are attempting to establish themselves as members of the congregation and are trying to find their places so they can move ahead. They are learning how to cope with community and are activity and structure oriented. As expected, they are much less reflective than midlife religious.

In the late 20s and early 30s, priests and religious are reaching the first adult transition. Some of their ideals about religious life and priesthood are shattered because of their overidealization of it. The result is discouragement and sometimes depression or acting out. Some question whether they want to stay and be the "workhorses" of a community with so few in their age group. The issue of intimacy is manifested in terms of their struggle for identity, to find their place in the community. This is particularly difficult for some where there may be a generation between them and the next youngest in the house. They are struggling for autonomy, which also becomes compounded in those communities with so few young people that they experience a generation gap, feel misunderstood, alienated, and judged by 40-year-old criteria. They are tired of being called the "kids" and want to be taken seriously by those in authority and others. Diocesan priests this age have trouble with pastors. Some therapists spoke of concern in the area of sexuality. One found considerable guilt related to masturbation and confusion about feelings for those of the same or the opposite sex. The area of sexual orientation is explored by some and they have to make a decision about a celibate or an active resolution. This age is a time of high intensity as people throw themselves into their work. Their energies are scattered and they become overextended, have no time for themselves and some even collapse and become depressed. This is frequently a time of greater stress than midlife.

What Is Your Experience With the Midlife Priests and Religious in Therapy?

The experience of the midlife priest and religious is very much what is described in the literature for any midlife person who is in touch with the transition. It is sometimes manifested by a mild depression and people ask, "What have I done with my life?" and "What am I doing now?" They take a serious look at the values that are most important to them in terms of personal and transcendent life-meaning and want to live the rest of their lives out of those values. Many are grieving the religious life-style that is over and are dealing with the disillusionment of the present and wondering if they should stay with what in their view may be a sinking ship. Women religious are seeking an identity apart from that of being the fourth grade teacher or whatever roll they fill. Career change is frequently part of the picture. As deeper values and the development of personal psychological and spiritual resources expand their interests the desire for other ministries emerges. Midlife people in therapy come from an experience of overwork if not workaholism and burnout, and diocesan priests in leadership positions feel pulled apart by the demands on their time and energy. This raises questions about loneliness, relationships, intimacy, friendship, community, and sexuality. For women sexuality is primarily an issue of affect and bonding; for men, it seems to be more one of genitality. Sexual orientation is sometimes an issue. Midlife priests and religious are searching for more balance in their lives. Several are dealing with aging parents, which, of course brings up issues of their own mortality.

Describe the Issues Which Come Up in Therapy With the Older Priest or Religious

Most therapists define a relatively small sample of the older person from age 60 to 70 or 80. One therapist, however, designated age 50-60 as a separate category in his practice with its own set of issues. Many women in this group have a "slush fund" of anger built up from the repressions of many years, because they held on to grudges and resentments. They are angry about missed opportunities and are envious of the advantages given to the young sisters. They are now taken for granted and are angry about that too. Much of their anger is justified in the therapist's view. Some go from the superdedicated worker to the somewhat lazy by comparison with past performance. They feel misunderstood. They do not know how to deal with anger or intimacy and become uptight and grumpy because of their resentments. Those over 60 may experience depression because of diminished energy which does not permit them to work as in the past. Some manifest adjustment reactions to physical decline and decreased health. Semi-retirement or retirement removes what was central to life. Some with long-term problems have run out of options within community. Many feel lonely and not appreciated and feel abandoned, especially by friends who left the order. They experience self-doubt and some undergo dark-night periods which refer to an inner spiritual darkness. There can be guilt over sexual issues of the past. Concerns about the life review, wondering whether they had made a mistake with their lives, and issues related to dying are brought up. One therapist found that his clients in this age group were mainly interested in one or two visits to help them to deal with a specific problem they were facing with day-to-day crises. Most in his practice do not continue in a therapeutic relationship.

Is the Religious Dimension an Issue of Therapy? If So, Could You Explain How It Comes Up and How You as a Therapist Process It?

All agreed that the religious dimension does come into therapy and that it is a very important area of exploration. All the therapists interviewed wait for the client to introduce it with the exception of one who said he would do so eventually just as he would the areas of relationship or sexuality if it never came up. Clients bring it up in terms of a faith crisis, doubt over their vocation which may involve a decision, life meaning, the experience of burnout where they wonder where the Spirit is, negative God images, an experience of a change in how they pray or an inability to pray, interpersonal conflict, the vows and how to live them out, guilt, fear of damnation, an inability to feel close to God, social responsibility, and growth in the integration of the spiritual in their daily lives, among others.

The therapists make a clear distinction between psychotherapy and spiritual direction which focuses on getting in touch with the action of God in the lives of people and their response to it. Some therapists will explore the psychological aspects of a religious issue only and will refer to a spiritual director. The House of Affirmation, a residential treatment center for priests and religious, has a Psychotheological Integration Group where residents can focus on the spiritual life, while individual sessions are clearly psychotherapeutic. Other therapists will work with these issues directly using the language mode of the client, that is, the language of psychology or of spirituality. In cases where a client uses spiritualized language as a defense, one therapist stated he avoids it entirely.

In many instances, when psychotherapists confront these issues, they are working with the underlying psychological ones. Negative God images frequently relate to difficulties with parents; anger and rage at God can be displaced anger at parents; the inability to feel close to God may relate to issues of intimacy; and the inability to pray may relate to the feeling that the client is falling apart psychologically. Some of the therapists noted that as people move along in the therapeutic process, the religious dimension becomes more prominent. One found that as women feel better about themselves and know themselves more, a feminine God image emerges. This is a God she can sit with in relationship and one who is gentle, non-imposing, loving, accepting, understanding, replacing the negative, judgmental masculine image they sometimes associate with priests.

How Does Community Life Emerge as a Therapeutic Issue?

It is a key issue. It affects personal life, prayer, and ministry. Those who become sexually involved are the men and women who have a poor community life. Diocesan priests particularly need to develop community supports.

One of the tensions within congregations is the diversity of local community styles which range from the traditional, where functional issues (Who does what?) are important, to the innovative, where interpersonal issues dominate. Therapists find that many clients have unrealistic expectations and think community life should fulfill the role of a spouse and family. They are not as aware as they might be of the need to share themselves with the community by physical presence: by reaching out to others, by pulling their weight in terms of work, and by being enriched elsewhere in order to nourish the community. Some clients describe themselves as marginal or fringe members of their communities, either by self-definition or that of the community. These members are of three types: (a) people in transition, for example, at early midlife or retirement, who are questioning how and where they fit; (b) people who have developed a high level of autonomy because of outside friends, professional attainment, life-style, or ministry; or are leadership types with many talents and are in fact committed to the community as congregation (some choose to put energies in ministry rather than in local living); and (c) the problem person with no place or friends inside or outside the community.

Clients frequently lack the skills for productive involvement in community such as skills in listening, conflict management, affirmation and confrontation, being able to be angry and to fight, and skills for the development of relationships. People are often "pegged" by community so that passive members who become more autonomous through therapy need to be integrated into the community in a new way. The House of Affirmation staff see a need for outreach to communities to help with this through systems therapy. Members in midlife who are being considered for leadership roles within the community question whether they should give a number of years to this at the cost of a viable ministry.

What Are the Advantages and/or Disadvantages to Your Being a Religious or a Lay Roman Catholic Psychotherapist?

The primary advantage is that the religious psychotherapist understands the life-style from within and the lay therapists interviewed understand it from long-term close association as well as their own religious commitment. This eliminates explanations about religious life as such. They can also appreciate the dramatic and traumatic differences between the pre and post Vatican II life-styles. There are shared values with the freedom to explore others, insights, and the capacity to be in touch with the nuances of contemporary issues within the Church as they affect people, for instance, women's issues. Some clients indicate they feel "safe" with therapists who "won't take away their faith" and with the extra assurance of confidentiality with a priest therapist.

On the negative side, the overidentification with the client may cause the therapist to assume too little or too much, and a tendency to moralize comes in occasionally. The "authority" the priest has to hear confessions may have a negative affect on some or the "superior" or the "all priests are alike" transference may get in the way of others.

Are You Implying That a Non-religious or a Non-Catholic Therapist Should Not Engage in Therapy With a Priest or Religious?

All would say emphatically "No." Some religious, priests, and lay Catholics would, in fact, not be good therapists at all for this population. What religious and priests look for is a therapist who respects their commitment, has a knowledge of community life, and an understanding of religious life and spirituality. Many therapists have refused to face this, in the opinion of some of those interviewed. Clients report enormous frustration at spending several hours of therapy educating the psycho-therapist about their life. Some therapists devalue religious life, or view it as neurotic, the source of the clients' problems, and encourage them to leave it. Some therapists have made suggestions negative to religious life and values, for example, masturbation, or have recommended "solu-tions" to issues at variance with their values which undercut their com-mitment and caused them to leave. Some of these former clients stated that they regretted that decision. Those who wish to work with this clien-tele need to acquire the necessary background and engage in some direct experiences with religious communities.

CONCLUSIONS

The developmental issues and struggles as well as the conflicts that bring other people to psychotherapy bring the religious and the priest. Some issues have their unique aspects because of their values and their life-styles. Some problems are exacerbated by the injunctions of a mis-understood and misappropriated religious dimension. The religious and spiritual dimension is significant for them and to ignore it is to render a great disservice to them since their lives are centered around this by vow, according to the therapists interviewed. The therapist who works with them needs to understand and respect this. One therapist noted that it is not only the people with problems that come to therapy, but also those in search of increased health as adults in relationship, work, and play. Con-cern about the integration of the spiritual and the psychological brings many, including younger people. This seems to reflect the experience of some therapists working with all kinds of people in search of meaning and values. Further exploration of therapy with religious and priests could of-fer valuable insights not only for future work with them but also for all those struggling with issues of spirituality and transcendence.

APPENDIX

Diocesan priest. A man ordained to serve the Church under the juris-diction of a bishop. He is involved in ministry to the people through ritual services, preaching, teaching, the administration of parishes, and other works for the service of the Church. In the Roman rite, he must take a vow of celibacy. He may live alone or with one or more other priests.

Ministry. The work done by a religious congregation or by individual members in the name of the Church for the good of others; for example, teaching, counseling, nursing, social services, and so forth.

Religious. A man or woman who is a member of a religious congregation bound by vows and sharing a common life. Male religious may be priests or brothers.

Religious community (also called order, institute, congregation, society). A group of people who sense a call from God and who share life together for their own spiritual growth and development and for the service of others according to the unique spirit of their founder.

A local community is a branch or small group of religious from the order situated in a city or parish to engage in ministry.

Superior. A member of a religious community who is the person in charge of other members of the community at the local level, the regional or provincial level, or congregational level.